America's Heritage:
Capitols of the United States

By
Willis J. Ehlert

America's Heritage: Capitols of the United States
By Willis J. Ehlert

State House Publishing
P.O. Box 5636
Madison, WI   53705

Printed in the United States by McNaughton & Gunn

Library of Congress Catalog Card Number   92-83705
ISBN 0-9634908-3-4

Published 1993

Dedication

To my wife who enjoyed the capitol visits with me and patiently encouraged and helped me with this project.

To our four children who grew up on our memorable summer camping trips and visited many of the capitols in our early travels.

Acknowledgment

When you begin to compile information and write a book, you have no idea the amount of help and counsel that you will need. Therefore, I wish to acknowledge and thank the real sources of much of the capitol and state information found in this book. The primary sources are the many state tourist and convention bureaus, state government offices, and the many individuals in those offices who provided so much help and information. Often when I visited a capitol, weather prevented taking satisfactory pictures or as often happened, renovation was taking place and prevented taking a good photograph. So a special thank you to those state agencies and individuals who provided many of the photographs of state capitols.

Effort has been made to provide accurate and concise information about the state capitols and state history. However, there may be mistakes in typographical and content that were not caught. Therefore, this book should be used only as a general guide and not as the final say in regards to capitols and history. Hopefully, all is accurate, but neither the author or publisher shall have liability or responsibility to anyone or any entity for liability or loss because of information contained in this book. The bibliography is accurate and current at the time of printing. Changes will occur and so neither the author or publisher can accept liability or responsibility for those changes.

Table of Contents

Preface

When I set out to do a book on state capitols, it was to be primarily a picture book with some basic information. In the past five years, the project grew to the point where I had to make a decision to restrict the text to fit the purposes of what I had in mind when I started. While there were several purposes for gathering and compiling the information found in the text of this book, the primary purpose was to provide basic information in one place about each state's capitol building that might be of interest to someone visiting the building or to students searching for basic information about their own capitals and capitol buildings.

Consequently, for each state, the first paragraph or two contain information about a state's Capitol building. This includes information about when it was built, what materials were used, and what prominent architectural features each building has. The other major purpose was to present a capsulation of each state's history so that someone visiting or wishing to learn the bare outline of a state's past, might be able to do so.

Finally, some basic information about a state's symbols, motto, and the origin of the state's name, is given in the final section. Someone reading the brief summary about each state and its capitol building should arrive at an understanding about the history of the state and how the capitol building came to be the seat of that state's government. The accompanying photographs present a panorama of the similarities and differences of the many capitol buildings. The appendix should add more insight to states' capitol histories. I wanted the bibliography to be more than the usual listing of source material so I've included addresses and phone numbers of state agencies that not only contributed to the research information but often provided photographs and other helps.

Hopefully, this book will provide a concise reference in one place that might be of use to students of U. S. history and others who desire information about their state. Perhaps the brief sketches will encourage them to learn more about their own state and capital as well as showing them the uniqueness of each state's Capitol building. Too often it is a laborious task to read the entire history of our country. We studied it in high school and really never considered it again. If the historical portions of each state are read at one sitting, the reader will gain a better knowledge of the progress of our country and become more aware of how each state contributed to in the formation of the United States of America.

For those who travel and who wish to capture some of the flavor of a state, a visit to the state's Capitol building will provide feeling for the state they are visiting. For example, a visit to the gray, volcanic-colored

7

Capitol building in Honolulu, Hawaii, built with columns resembling stately palm trees, with its great open center suggesting a volcanic crater, will provide a feeling of ambiance that says "Hawaii." Or a visit to Oklahoma's traditional Capitol would perhaps not be memorable except that the flavor of the state is conveyed by the capital complex having an oil derrick near the front steps of the Capitol building. Again, there are many other memorable identification points that mark the capitol buildings. The Bulfinch designed Massachusetts Capitol with its gold dome is one such memorable identification point. The ornate, gold-domed Iowa capitol with its four smaller domes is another. The Dutch Gothic chateau-like appearance of the New York capitol building is unique. When approaching Lincoln, Nebraska, on Interstate 80, the sudden appearance in the distance of the 400 foot skyscraper capitol, rising against the sky like a beacon, is a sight that remains memorable and one that is looked forward to each time I-80 is traveled. The list of memorable points about each capitol building could include all fifty.

What is suggested to the reader, is that as you travel about this diverse land of ours, visit as many of the capitols as you can. You will find the visits memorable stops on your journey. The bibliography includes current state tourist and information addresses and telephone numbers. Writing and/or calling will get the interested person the particular state's tourist information packet. State agencies provide a plethora of material and information about their most important state building. They take pride in their states' showplaces and provide helpful guides and information about their state capitol.

Over the past forty years, some of the most fascinating places that we have visited have been forty-five of the fifty state capitol buildings. It is hoped that this book will convey the uniqueness of each of the capitol buildings in the United States. So go out and enjoy the United States, enjoy the states, and enjoy their unique Capitols! They are well worth a visit!

Willis J. Ehlert

Introduction

Throughout history man has sought a center of government from which to focus his ruling instincts. At some point in his history when man decided to govern himself and the society he belonged to, he began to focus on a government center. Undoubtedly the first cave dweller chosen to lead his people, established his cave as a center of government. As man developed more structured societies, he began to form dictatorial, oligarchical, monarchal, or democratic governments that needed centers from which governing could occur. Most often the display of power to govern took the outward physical form of structures that announced this power. Initially, it probably was the tribal chief's place of residence, but in order to give credence to his rule, man began to embellish this residence. Eventually it became the largest structure around, filled with symbols, announcing that this was the residence housing the ruler or rulers and the governing bodies. In ancient times, the city state of Athens with its Acropolis, where the ruling family lived, probably established this principle for all time. The Athenian government buildings with the architectural forms that were developed have been copied and modified in government buildings up to the present time. Later from the Norman Conquest of England with the moot and bailey castles that William the Conqueror established across England to the Crusader castles built in Turkey and to the European medieval period with the manors and castles housing an area's ruler, the castle became not only a means of defense, but it functioned as a seat of government for the king who ruled over the entire country or the lord who ruled over an area. These city states, towns, and castles became the capital of a designated area so that there was some consolidation and some formal structure to carry on the role of governing. Often groups of advisors became attached to the ruler and advised upon courses of action. In a sense, these were the first governing bodies or legislatures.

The need to construct imposing and authoritative structures as centers of government seems then to be a part of man's nature as he adjusted to changing social conditions. Ancient Rome was such a place. All life and all men looked toward Rome as the center from 50 B.C. to 450 AD. Constructed in the center of Rome were buildings more grandiose than the common man could imagine. Their existence announced to the world that here was situated the power to rule peoples' lives. These complexes of government buildings, constructed and added to by a succession of rulers, served to announce to the world a ruler's authority and acted as a remembrance of past rulers' reigns.

"Capitol" is derived from the Roman Capitoline Hill, where the Temple of Jupiter was built above the Roman Forum, the center of Roman government. "Capitol" became fixed in American law when it was used to designate the Williamsburg government building for the Virginia colony. It was the first large government building to house an American legislature.

Today, Washington, D. C. is such a place with the Capitol building the center of government buildings where government takes place. Along with these buildings, we have constructed remembrances to our past history and past rulers. Examples are the Washington monument, the Lincoln and Jefferson Memorials, the Marine Memorial, and the Vietnam Memorial Wall.

The need to present an authoritative posture to the common man and to the future was not confined to the secular only. The sacred communities from the monasteries of Tibet to the Medieval cathedrals in Europe used large, imposing structures as a seat of sacred authority. Structures such as St. Peters in Rome, Notre Dame in Paris, the Mosques at Mecca and the Hagia Sophia in Istanbul, are or were the centers of religious authority and the buildings in these places show this authority. Although past civilizations are remembered historically, their buildings remain to convey a permanence and grand design for which the civilization stood.

The architectural tradition then of constructing government buildings of permanence stretches back in man's history to early civilizations and is today carried on in the United States in our National Capitol and our states' capitol buildings. While a majority of the present capitol buildings were constructed during the 19th. and 20th. centuries and were the result of a need for larger quarters and a more permanent seat of government, all were built to convey this permanence to the people that are governed and are the repositories of a states's history through paintings, statues, and symbols. The capitol became the dominant symbol of government authority.

However, this was not always the situation. Early in our nation's history most capitol buildings were more utilitarian with wood as the primary building material. Early capitol buildings such as the wooden carpenter built ones in Austin, Texas; St. Paul, Minnesota; Salem, Oregon; and Tallahassee, Florida, were almost temporary structures lasting only a few decades. Today the carpenter built Florida Capitol is a museum and can be seen as it was in 1909. Other states have been able to preserve early capitol buildings. One excellent example of an early Capitol building that was not constructed of wood is the imposing solid Greek Revival style building in Springfield, Illinois, situated only a short way from today's Illinois State Capitol building. The old Capitol is a repository of Abraham Lincoln memorabilia with the highlight a President Lincoln handwritten copy of his "Gettysburg Address."

Another early capitol building that has been preserved is the early Arkansas Capitol building located in Little Rock, again just a short distance from today's Capitol. Completed in 1842, it is an excellent example of Classical Doric architecture. Inside, many rooms have been restored to middle 19th. century condition, displaying Victorian furniture, furnishings, clothing, and historical objects from that period.

Iowa's Doric styled Greek Revival first State Capitol in Iowa City was designed by John F. Rague, who also designed Illinois' old capitol building. Today it is a museum of state history located in center of the campus of the University of Iowa. When Iowa's capital was moved to Des Moines, the structure was used for a time by the University of Iowa as the administration building. Today all rooms have been restored to the 1840's when Iowa gained statehood. A prominent feature of the interior is the elegant, reverse, free standing spiral staircase in the center of the building. An unusual feature of this rare type of stairs is that the top step is directly over the bottom step.

The national mind-set for Classical Greek Revival architecture was a major part of 19th. century American thinking. Here was a young nation that was striving to establish itself in the world of nations. Here was a new nation, carved out of the wilderness, with a crude, rudimentary civilization having no traditions. What better image to convey to other more established nations than that of a nation that revered and cherished the architectural traditions of the past?

Consequently, 19th. century designers of the National Capitol and state capitols turned to what they considered historical permanence, classical architecture. During the years from 1800-1969, we built twenty-two capitol buildings in the 19th. century and twenty-five in the 20th. century. Most of these were constructed soon after state governments were formalized and certainly all are the reflection of the way in which the people of a state wanted the rest of society to view them. The time span of the capitols is from the classical Thomas Jefferson designed Richmond State House of 1800 to the 1932 Cass Gilbert designed domed classical Renaissance, West Virginia Capitol in Charleston, to the stylized Hawaiian Capitol built in 1969 in Honolulu. Capitol architects' designs ranged from the colonial styled Capitol at Dover, Delaware, to the thirty-four classical Greek-Roman styled domed capitols; from the modern skyscraper at Baton Rouge, Louisiana, built in 1932, to the modern stylistic Indian influenced Capitol at Santa Fe, New Mexico, built in 1967. Each was done with the intention of establishing the appearance of permanence

11

in government in the heritage of the past.

The concept, then, of a territorial or state capitol as a focus for a seat of government is one that is embedded in history. As each of the territories in the United States became a state, a site was designated as the seat of government or capital. Often territorial designated capitals were only temporary and in time were passed by as settlement dictated that the capital of a state be moved to a more formal location and a capitol building constructed. Wisconsin is a prime example of this change. Belmont was established as the first territorial capital, but later the capital was moved to Madison. Belmont today is a small hamlet while Madison is a city of over 190,000.

Quite often a capital was not moved, and the city is noted primarily for its governmental role. Examples of this are Frankfort, Kentucky; Salem, Oregon; Helena, Montana; and Carson City, Nevada. Often before a permanent seat of government was established, representatives of the people from various towns and areas would travel around and meet in different locations. For example, until 1808, Vermont representatives met 46 times in 14 different towns. North Carolina representatives met in several towns until the capital was established at Raleigh in 1792. Therefore, the natural progression to locate a permanent place for meeting was a easy decision and another reason for establishing a capital and building a capitol building.

However, it was a decision that often brought on political crises. Our history is filled with political strife about the location of a state capital. In fact, we have several more states than we might have had if locating a capital had been easy. For example, a dispute over the location of the capital of the Dakota territory when statehood was discussed, was resolved with the Dakota territory being divided into the states of North and South Dakota on November 2, 1889.

The Civil War, perhaps more than any other event in our history, brought about several new states because of regional differences. West Virginia is one example. Support for the Confederate cause by coastline Virginians, drove the inland residents of Virginia to form a new state that was admitted to the Union in 1863 as West Virginia. Earlier in 1820, the Missouri Compromise continued a balance of free and slave states in the Senate when Missouri and Maine were admitted together. Location of a capitol building was a political dispute among the residents of Columbus, Ohio, when an influential group decided to locate the capitol building across the river from the original county seat and away from where most of the population was located. So the establishing of a capital and in some cases, a capitol building, was often a cause for dispute and compromise in our history.

Architecturally, the American capitol building and its site follow a well defined tradition for construction and setting. The capitol is usually located in the center of a terrace that surrounds or fronts a building. Most often the building is built on a hill, high mound or high point in the city where it is located in much the same fashion as the castles which were often located on higher ground than the surrounding countryside. This can most dramatically be seen in the locations of the Tennessee Capitol in Nashville, in the Kentucky Capitol in Frankfort, and in the Capitol of Utah in Salt Lake City. These and many other capitol buildings are built on high ground and overlook the city. Many of the thirty-four domed classical capitol buildings took as a model for layout and appearance the United States Capitol building in Washington, D. C. This model for the bicameral legislature with its impressive domed building became the standard for architects designing state capitols.

Capitol buildings by their appearance convey a permanence to the people who are governed. The buildings generally are laid out on the same plan with some variations. There is the central rotunda, rising up to a view of the interior of the dome, where a painting is often exhibited. On each side of the rotunda are the two balanced wings for the legislature and senate rooms. Often the judicial and executive are in two other wings off a central hall. Certainly variations of the classic Italian Renaissance dome on thirty-four capitols indicates the importance that people felt about giving their capitol building a sense of historical permanence.

Capitols are an embodiment of the period when they were constructed as well as a show place for what a state has to offer. Most are repositories of a state's history depicted through portraits and statues, and with idealized art presentations that depict the values, industry, and culture of a state. From the many circular paintings on rotunda ceilings to the numerous large murals in rotundas and in the legislative and judicial chambers, capitol buildings are impressive art museums.

A fine example is Kansas' Capitol at Topeka. The paintings of Kansas history by noted American artist, John Steuart Curry, rival those found in any art gallery. His dramatic painting of abolitionist John Brown, set against a tumultuous Kansas background, is often considered his greatest painting and a masterpiece depicting the conflict between free and slave states. Rhode Island's Capitol holds early American portrait paintings including Gilbert Stuart's portrait of George Washington standing by his desk. The Virginia Capitol at Richmond displays probably the most priceless marble statue in the United States, a life size statue of George Washington created by Jean Antoine Houdon.

To experience a sense of a state's history and culture is one of the reasons for visiting our state capitols. Often the capitol building itself is a

13

reflection of the unique culture from which the state was created. A prime example of this is the unusual Indian kiva-styled building that is the New Mexico Capitol. Upon entering a state capitol, the viewer is struck by the elegance of the gleaming marble often found in capitol buildings. Some, however, are more utilitarian and have used more modern materials such as concrete and building stone. Hawaii's use of concrete to convey the color and the texture of volcanic lava and yet create a striking and unique structure is such an example. All, regardless of construction, present a formality and a solemnity that conveys the serious governmental functions that are conducted in the building as a state's seat of government.

Today state capitol buildings are a true link with our historical past as well as our link to the future. They are symbols of a free people caught up in the human enterprise of governing themselves democratically. Through the architecture, the decorative interiors, the works of art, and the democratic function of government that occurs daily, the Capitols of the United States are truly America's Heritage.

The Capitol
of the
United States

The Capitol of the United States

When George Washington took the oath of office for President on April 30, 1789, he did so in New York then the temporary capital of the United States. During the early years of the Republic, there was much rivalry among cities as to which should be chosen as the center of government. In a move to prevent continued rivalry, Congress passed the Residency Act of 1790 that provided for a separate site on which to build a new city to house the capital. Ten square miles along the Potomac River between Maryland and Virginia were ceded to the federal government by those states for the construction of a city that would become the center of government.

The French engineer, Major Pierre Charles L'Enfant, known to George Washington, was chosen to design the new city. L'Enfant had studied architecture at the Royal Academy of Paris where he was influenced by Le Notre's plan for Versailles. In 1791, his plan was to create a capitol building and a President's house set in midst of parks and wide avenues. He chose an eighty-eight foot plateau that dominated the city of Washington as the site for the capitol. In 1793, competition for design of the capitol building was held and Dr. William Thornton, an amateur architect, won, designing a stately building in a classical style.

Thornton's classically styled structure would be a building with a central dome and with identical wings on each side. George Washington laid the cornerstone for the Capitol on September 18, 1793. However, construction was slow and a succession of architects did sections of the Capitol. Seven years passed and only the north wing under the direction of James Hoban and Stephen Hallet had been completed by 1800. The south wing was completed seven years later under architect, Benjamin H. Latrobe. On August 24, 1814, during the War of 1812, the British burned the Capitol. In 1815, Latrobe began the reconstruction. By 1824, the domed portion between the wings was completed under the direction of Charles Bulfinch. He designed a higher wooden dome than Thornton's original based upon the Pantheon in Rome. The center section of the Capitol is built of Virginia limestone but the two wings built in 1851 under the direction of Robert Mills who was later dismissed by President Fillmore in 1851, are built of white Massachusetts marble.

Adding the two wings threw off the building's proportions when seen with the older bowl-like dome of Bulfinch, so in 1854-5, the present hemispherical dome, constructed of cast iron, was designed by Thomas

Ustick Walter of Philadelphia. Walter's plans were for a new huge dome over the central rotunda that would balance out and be more in proportion with the two added wings. The design was selected by President Millard Fillmore. Construction of the enlargement of the Capitol and the huge dome, which when completed would be for a time the largest use of cast iron in any building in the world, was begun in 1851, revised, and completed in 1863. Walter used a trussed iron frame that would carry interior and external shells of cast iron panels thus making a lighter weight dome than one made of masonry.

Because Walter had to stay within the parameters of Thornton's dome and because he wanted to create a tall, eye-pleasing dome, he turned to the Renaissance dome and designed a steep, high dome with influences from St. Peter's in Rome, the Pantheon in Paris, St. Paul's in London, and St. Issac in St. Petersburg. Its height in the 1859 design is 218 feet The dome's base diameter is 135 feet, 5 inches. The wide skirt or base supports the drum, consisting of the first story set behind the peristyle of 36 Corinthian columns. Upon the peristyle is the lower balustrade and second story with its decorative pilasters. Above the pilasters is a ring of consoles comprising the attic. Over the attic is the 35 foot, quarter inch main dome or cupola that arches upward toward the second and smaller balustrade that is a part of the tholos or lantern housing with its Corinthian columns. Set upon this housing is the pedestal upon which is set Thomas Crawford's 19 foot, 6 inch statue of "Freedom." The figure wears a crested helmet and from a distance it is often mistaken for a war bonneted Indian warrior. Total height from ground level to the top of the Freedom statue is 287 feet, 6 inches.

The columns on the porticoes of the front of the main building and on the front of the two legislative structures on either side are of the Corinthian order. The pilastered walls between the wings are Corinthian order as well. The entire structure is surmounted by an entablature and a balustrade parapet. The central section and both wings have double porticoes supported by Corinthian columns. Each supports a pediment with different marble tableaux, some of the finest examples of American sculpturing. For example, the Senate north pediment has Thomas Crawford's "Progress of American Civilization and the Decline of the Indian." The House south pediment displays Paul Bartlett's "Peace Protecting Genius," one of the finest of American sculptures. The ten foot bronze doors leading from the central portico to the rotunda, display the "Story of Christopher Columbus" done by Randolph Rogers.

These exterior art works are only the beginning of the multitude of art works that the Capitol contains. Inside the building are over 300 pieces of paintings and sculpture. The circular rotunda under the central dome is an immense 95 feet 8 inches in diameter and rises 183 feet to the central

18

dome. The walls are Virginia sandstone and are divided by fluted Doric pilasters. Huge oil paintings grouped about the walls commemorate the major events of the young country's historic beginnings.

Events commemorated are "Embarkation of the Pilgrims" by Robert Weir, John Vanderlyn's famous "Landing of Columbus" and John Trumbull's scenes from the Revolutionary War. One of the most striking and certainly the most famous is Trumbull's "Signing of the Declaration of Independence." Adding to the total art experience in the rotunda are the many statues of famous Americans done by prominent sculptors. The huge 4,464 square foot painting on the ceiling high above the floor entitled the "Apotheosis of Washington" painted by Constantino Brumidi completes the total environment of art in the Capitol.

Completed at the end of the Civil War, the National Capitol became a symbol of the strength and preservation of the Union. Even though materials were in short supply because of the Civil War, Lincoln stated that the dome was to be completed because it would be a sign that the Union would continue. Today the 751 foot 4 inch long, 350 foot wide Capitol consists of seven units surmounted by the great iron dome that is painted white to match the building's masonry.

Because the U. S. Capitol became a symbol of legislative governing to U. S. citizens, a total of twenty-five state capitols constructed after the Civil War used the Capitol in Washington, D.C. as a model. Prominent among the designers of state capitol who did this were Cass Gilbert, designer of the Capitols of Minnesota and West Virginia, Elijah E. Meyers, designer of the Capitol buildings of Colorado, Michigan, and Texas, and John C. Cochrane, designer of the Iowa and Illinois Capitol buildings.

The United States Capitol building remains today the world's most recognizable symbol of the democratic government that is housed inside. The structure is the culmination of the revival of Classical architecture with its Classical-Renaissance pillars and majestic Renaissance dome.

State Capitols
of the
United States

State Capitols of the United States

Wisconsin's Roman styled dome has all the elements of Classical architecture: lantern housing with the gilded bronze "Wisconsin," Corinthian columns supporting the drum that holds the dome, a series of balustrade railings on on two levels, and Ionic columns with a dentil encirclement above.

The gables on New York's Romanesque-Gothic styled Capitol display base-relief figures and arched-covered windows.

The very ornate Texas State Capitol front has many classical features such as an arched entrance, pilasters, and topped by a pediment.

The Michigan Capitol legislative rooms have intricate ceilings with glass panels displaying the states' seals.

Maine's Capitol has simple, elegant Classical lines with an unadorned pediment supported by Tuscan columns

Alabama

The Cotton State

Alabama's State Capitol building, located in downtown Montgomery on a site called "Goat's Hill," was completed in 1851 to replace the original capitol building which burned on December 14, 1849, two years after its completion as soon after the state capital was moved from Tuscaloosa to Montgomery.

The Capitol building of stucco over brick is in the Greek revival style with six Corinthian columns on each of the facades. The hemispherical dome is supported by Corinthian columns surrounding the drum. A prominent feature of the building is the 20 day clock, "The City of Montgomery Clock," over the front portico. The interior of the dome has paintings by Roderick MacKernzie depicting events in Alabama's history. A dominant feature of the rotunda are the two cantilevered spiral staircases rising three stories above the floor.

This historic structure hosted Alabama's secession convention and housed the first Confederate Congress. It served as the capital of the Confederacy during the first few months of the Civil War. A brass star on the top of the steps of the west portico of the Capitol marks the spot where Jefferson Davis was sworn in as president of the Confederate government.

State History

Spanish exploration of the area took place first under Hernando de Soto in 1539. Indian tribes under the direction of Chief Tuscaloosa or Black Warrior, fought the Spanish and continued to battle them for the next century and a half. Finally in 1763, when the Treaty of Paris that concluded the French and Indian War was signed, the area became a British possession. Spain waited until the American Revolution to assert itself, and finally made a settlement with the new United States government in 1795. The agreed upon border, the 31st. parallel, remained until the Louisiana Purchase in 1803, made the Alabama area part of the United States.

During the War of 1812, the Creek Indians, encouraged by the British, rose up under Tecumsah, and massacred settlers at Fort Mims. General Andrew Jackson defeated them in the Creek Wars. Following this victory, thousands of settlers entered the territory and in a few short years, Alabama entered the Union on December 14, 1819, as the 22nd. state. Following statehood, Tuscaloosa became the capital and remained the capital until 1846, when Montgomery became the permanent capital. The question of slavery in the state was addressed by the States' Right wing of the Democratic Party, when John C. Calhoun led a delegation that supported the "Alabama Platform" in 1848. It stated that the Federal government could not interfere in territorial internal affairs. In 1861, the Ordinance of Secession was passed and Montgomery became the capital of the Confederacy. By the year 1865, most of Alabama was in Union hands. Following the war, reconstruction brought Alabama under martial law until 1868, when the state ratified the Fourteen Amendment. Federal troops were withdrawn in 1876, and self-government returned to Alabama.

State Symbols

The state bird is the Yellowhammer; the state flower is the camellia; the state tree is the Longleaf pine. The official dance is the square dance. The fresh water fish is the Largemouth bass; the salt water fish, the tarpon. Marble is the official rock; hematite, the mineral. The state nut is the pecan. Alabama's fossil is *basilosaurus cetoides*; its horse, the rocking horse. The Cotton State's motto is "We Dare Defend Our Rights." The name Alabama comes from two Choctaw Indian words meaning "thicket clearers."

Alaska

The Last Frontier State

The Alaskan State Capitol, set against the background of the majestic Coast Mountains, is located in downtown Juneau. The Capitol building is a six-story structure of the modern office building type. It is made of brick-faced reinforced concrete with the lower facade of Indiana limestone. The four columns of the portico and the interior trim are of light and dark Tokeen marble from the quarries at Tokeen, Prince of Wales Island, Alaska. The building was begun on September 18, 1929, completed February 2, 1931, and dedicated on February 14, 1931. It originally was the Federal and Territorial Building which served as headquarters for the Territory of Alaska.

State History

Modern Alaskan history begins with Russian explorers from Siberia reaching the Alaskan mainland sometime in the 18th. century. In 1728, Vitus Bering, a Dane employed by Russia, navigated the strait named after him. He later returned in 1741, stayed, and died on the mainland. Members of the Russian explorers led by Chirikoff, who had arrived with Bering, took furs back to Russia and as a result brought a rush of Russian fur hunters and traders. By 1799, Russia had set up the Russian-American Fur Company. Russia made no attempt to colonize the area and most of the interior remained undeveloped or relatively unexplored until the U. S. purchased Alaska.

The U. S. had attempted to purchase the area in 1857 and failed, but it was Secretary of State William Seward who resumed negotiations with Russia for the purchase after the Civil War. The negotiations resulted in a treaty of purchase signed in Washington on March 30, 1867. The price was $7,200,000. Throughout the century it was ridiculed as Seward's Folly. In the early years after the purchase, there was little activity except for seal hunting. The gold rush to the Klondike occurred in 1896 and the view of Alaska changed. Population grew and years of struggle to gain statehood followed. The first Senate vote in 1952, failed, but in 1959, statehood was approved and it became the 49th. state on January 3, 1959.

State Symbols

The Great Seal of Alaska depicts the state's motto, "North to the Future." Alaska's state bird is the Willow Ptarmigan; its flower is the forget-me not; its tree, the Sitka Spruce. The state fish is the King salmon; the marine mammal the Bowhead whale. The state gem is jade; its mineral, gold. The state sport is dog mushing. The name "Alaska" is said to perhaps derive from the Aleut word meaning "mainland" or from the Eskimo word signifying "great country."

Arizona

The Grand Canyon State

Arizona's unique State Capitol, located in downtown Phoenix, is today the Arizona State Capitol Museum. Like many other state capitols, it first served as the Territorial Capitol from 1901 to 1912 and later as the State Capitol. The Capitol building, constructed between 1898 and 1901, was designed by James Reily Gordon of San Antonio, Texas. The building is constructed of native Arizona stone. The walls are tufa stone from Skull Valley with malapa from the Camelback Mountains used in the foundation. Gray granite from the Salt River Mountains used on the first floor. In 1976, the low, tin dome was covered with gleaming copper donated by the state copper industry.

A prominent feature of the building is the quarter-ton, 16 foot high sculptured weather vane titled "Winged Victory" which crowns the copper dome. She holds a torch aloft. The distance from the floor to the tip of the torch is ninety-two feet, six inches. Ionic columns support a decorative pediment on the portico over the arched entrances. Today the Capitol Building, listed on the National Register of Historic Places, is an official museum with state business conducted in an office building directly behind the museum.

State History

Around 1535-36, Cabeza de Vaca became the first European to explore the Arizona area when he touched upon it on his way to Mexico. In 1539, Marcos de Niza, a Franciscan missionary led by Estebanico, who had been with de Vaca, explored the area. Their reports brought Francisco de Coronado the following year, and the Spanish influence was established. The next centuries saw little settlement because of the Indian presence and the constant wars between them and the Spanish. In 1821, Spain ceded the area to Mexico. Then at the end of the Mexican War in 1848, the United States received the territory.

With the discovery of gold in California, there was a need for the U. S. to have a clear route to the coast. This need resulted in the Gadsden Purchase in 1854, fixing the international boundary between the U. S. and Mexico. During the Civil War, the area became the Confederate Territory of Arizona, but by 1862, it was in Union control and Lincoln approved the act creating the Arizona Territory on February 24, 1863. The railroad brought settlers and ranching replaced the Wild West in the later part of the 19th. century. After years of political maneuvering which had President Taft vetoing the act to make Arizona a state, the Arizona Territory finally became the 48th. state on February 14, 1912.

State Symbols

The Arizona's state flower is the blossom of the Saguaro cactus; its bird is the Cactus Wren; its tree, the Paloverde. The state gem is turquoise; its neckwear, the bola tie. Arizona's motto "God Enriches" reflects its early history of missionary explorers. The name Arizona comes from the Pagago Indian word meaning, "little spring."

Arkansas

Land of Opportunity

Arkansas' traditional Greek Revival Capitol building with its Renaissance styled dome and three Ionic style four-columned porticoes is located in Little Rock. It was constructed between 1899 and 1915 on the site of the former state penitentiary. The Capitol's interior is marble from Vermont, Colorado, and Alabama. The exterior of the building is "Arkansas marble," a limestone quarried near Batesville.

Unique features of the Capitol are the Tiffany chandeliers and the four inch thick Tiffany brass doors on the East front. The Greek Ionic style is displayed by the columns supporting the pediment over the front entrance and the matching two side porticoes. The dome drum is supported by a colonnade of twenty-four Ionic columns. A single gold ball sets atop the lantern housing. The largest Tiffany chandelier hangs from the center of the 185 foot high dome interior and weighs two ton. Small Tiffany chandeliers are hanging in the Senate and House chambers. Before the construction of the Capitol building, Arkansas' governmental bodies like those in many other states, met in various places in the state following entrance into the Union on June 15, 1836, as the 25th. state.

State History

The first European explorer to visit the site of Arkansas was Hernando de Soto in 1541, but it was Marquette and Joliet who in 1673, opened the region to further exploration as they journeyed down the Mississippi River. La Salle claimed the territory for France in 1682. The first permanent settlement was by the French under Henri de Tonti in 1686 at Arkansas Post on the Arkansas River. The area was ceded to Spain by France in 1762, then back to France in 1800 in the treaty of San Ildefonso.

The U. S. acquired the territory as part of the Louisiana Purchase in 1803. It became a territory in 1819 with the capital established at Little Rock in 1821. Although there was a strong pro-Union following in Arkansas, it entered the Union as a slave state. On May 6, 1861, Arkansas seceded from the Union to fight with the Confederacy. Many battles were fought within the state as Union and Confederate forces battled for supremacy of the area. The conclusion came when Little Rock was captured by the Union in 1863. Arkansas was readmitted to the Union on June 23, 1868.

State Symbols

The state flower is apple blossom; its bird, the mockingbird; the tree, the shortleaf pine; and the official insect, the honeybee. The state gem is the diamond; the mineral, quartz crystal, and the rock, bauxite. Milk is the state drink; the fiddle, the instrument. Arkansas is named for Arkansas Indian tribe of the Sioux Indians. The state's motto, "The People Rule," reflects the state's democratic background.

The Old State House of Arkansas opened in 1836. Today it is a historical museum.

California

The Golden State

California's magnificent domed Capitol was built in the years 1861-78. Set in a park of ten city blocks, it is surrounded by over 400 varieties of exotic trees and plants and is the oldest capitol west of the Mississippi River. It is highlighted by the eight Roman Corinthian columns on its front portico and a copper-clad wooden sheathed dome that is 220 feet high. The dome is supported by a compounded drum with the first tier a colonnade of Corinthian columns and the second tier of modified

Corinthian pilasters. It is topped by a thirty inch gold-covered ball set atop a twelve columned lantern housing with a small dome. The Capitol's base is gray granite from Folsom. Later when the Central Pacific Railroad reached Rochlin and a lighter granite was quarried and used. The capitol's exterior is brick set in lime mortar and covered with plaster. The interior features a 120' high rotunda. A highlight on the main floor is a Carrara marble statue carved in 1871, in Florence, Italy, entitled, "Columbus' Last Appeal to Queen Isabella."

State History

In 1540, Hernando de Alarcon, searching for the Seven Cities of Cibola, was the first explorer to visit California. California was later explored by European explorers, Juan Cabrillo in 1542 and by Sir Francis Drake in 1579. The first settlement was the Spanish Mission founded by Franciscan Father Junipero Serra at San Diego in 1769. Father Serra and Father Fermin Lasuen each continued to establish missions about a day's journey apart as they moved northward up the California coast. Altogether twenty-one missions were constructed along the road northward that became known as "El Camino Real."

California territory became a part of Mexico after Mexico declared its independence from Spain in 1822. In 1839, John Sutter arrived and developed an agricultural empire. He purchased the Russian land at Fort Ross in 1841 and the Russians left the area. California was a part of Mexico until 1848 when it was ceded to the U. S. after U. S. troops occupied the territory in 1846 as a part of the Mexican War which ended in 1848 with the Treaty of Guadalupe Hildalgo. Gold was discovered at Sutter's Fort in Sacramento in 1848 and the resultant Gold Rush help to populate the Western seacoast. On September 9, 1850, California became the 32nd. state as a free state. The completion of the Transcontinental Railroad in 1869 linked California to the rest of the U. S.

State Symbols

California's state bird is the Valley Quail; its flower is the Golden Poppy that is seen along the roads in summer; the tree is the California Redwood. The California grizzly bear is the state animal; the Golden trout, the state fish. Its insect is the California dog-face butterfly; the marine mammal, the gray whale. The reptile is the California desert tortoise. Its state mineral is gold; its rock, serpentine. The state's motto reflects the promised land that is California, "Eureka, I have found it." The name "California" probably came from a 16th. century Spanish romance that describes an island, Californian, inhabited by Amazons.

Colorado

The Centennial State; The Silver State

The Colorado Capitol building in Denver is designed on an axis in the form of a Greek Cross and resembles the basic Classical design of the nation's Capitol in Washington, D. C. Like so many capitol buildings, Colorado's, begun in 1886, was not completed until many years after becoming a state. The Capitol's construction took twenty-two years to complete because the builders were determined to use mostly state materials.

The Capitol's six front portico columns supporting the classical pediment are Corinthian. The outer walls are Gunnison granite; the foundations, Fort Collins sandstone; the floors and stairs are marble from the town of Marble; and the wainscoting is the exquisite rose onyx from Beulah, the only area in the world where the rose onyx is found. Its gold-covered dome rises 272 feet above the ground. Inside, the rotunda rises 180 feet above the floor. Inside the dome are sixteen stained glass windows portraying Colorado pioneers. Another interior feature is the Grand Staircase encrusted with oak leaves and acorns and consisting of seventy-seven marble steps and 175 brass balustrades.

State History

The Cliff Dwellers were the first inhabitants to leave a record of their activities in the Colorado area. Francisco Coronado was probably the first European explorer in the area in 1541 when he passed through on his return to Mexico after searching northward for the Seven Cities of Cibola. Other Spanish explorers and missionaries seeking a route to California followed in the next two centuries.

The Colorado area was further explored in the 1800's by Zebulon Pike in 1806 and by Stephen Long in 1820. Later John Fremont and mountain men followed. A portion of the state was acquired by the U. S. in the Louisiana Purchase in 1803, and the remaining parts came with the acquisition of Texas in the Treaty of Guadalupe Hildago ending the Mexican War in 1848. It was the discovery of gold and silver in 1858 that brought thousands of settlers to the area.

In 1861, the territory of Colorado was formed from Kansas, Nebraska, New Mexico, and Utah territories. Settlers in the territory fought on the Union side during the Civil War. In 1867, Denver was selected as the permanent seat of territorial government, but before that Colorado City, now part of Colorado Springs, and later Golden City were the territorial headquarters. Colorado was admitted to the Union on August 1, 1876, as the 38th. state.

State Symbols

Colorado's state bird is the lark bunting; its flower is the Rocky Mountain columbine; its tree, the Colorado blue spruce. The state animal is the Rocky Mountain bighorn sheep. Its gem is aquamarine. Colorado's state motto is "Nothing Without Providence." The name Colorado comes from the Spanish word "colorado" meaning "colorful" referring to the brownish-red color of the Colorado river at flood-stage.

Connecticut

The Constitution State; Nutmeg State

The imposing Connecticut State Capitol in Hartford is a prime example of Neo-Gothic architecture style which flourished in the U. S. during the 19th. century. Until 1873, Hartford had shared the honor as Connecticut's capital with New Haven, but a popular referendum in that year made Hartford the permanent capital. Constructed in the late 19th. century, the Capitol building became the official state capitol in 1879 when the state legislature met for their first regular session in the Capitol building.

The ornate, marble and granite building, features four towers and two Gothic style wings that present figures and ornamentation across its entire feudal appearing exterior. The exterior marble is from East Canaan, Connecticut, and the building's granite is from Rhode Island. Its gold-leafed dome is ringed by twelve figures representing Agriculture, Commerce, Education, Science, Music, and Force. Historical subjects such as the famed Charter Oak are pictured in base relief in the facades over the doorways.

In the interior of the building are three sky-lit wells enclosed on three levels by connecting balconies. The court yard like openings are graced by hand-painted columns, stenciled beams, and Italian marbled floors. On the first floor is the statue of Connecticut's hero, Nathan Hale.

State History

While Connecticut was first explored by Adriaen Block, a Dutch navigator, in 1614, it was the English Puritans from Massachusetts who made the first permanent settlements in 1633 near Windsor. That same year the Dutch built a fort at Hartford. The name "Constitution State" is given Connecticut because they declared the first democratic government in their Fundamental Orders of 1639, a document that is based on the will of the people from the towns of Hartford, Windsor, and Wethersfield. For over a hundred years, the colony was basically an oligarchy ruled by the Congregationalists.

By the Revolutionary War, laws were more liberal and all enjoyed freedom of religion. The state's Colonial governor, Jonathan Trumbull, was the only Colonial governor that supported the Revolution, providing provisions to George Washington's troops. Connecticut was the first colony to adopt the Declaration of Independence. During the Revolutionary War the British destroyed many of Connecticut's cities and citizens. Connecticut was the fifth of the thirteen original colonies to ratify the Constitution on January 9, 1788. During the Civil War, Connecticut exceeded its quota, sending six regiments to the support of the Union.

State Symbols

Connecticut's state bird is the robin; its flower, the mountain laurel; and its tree is the white oak. The state animal is the sperm whale; its insect, the praying mantis. Connecticut's mineral is garnet. It has a state ship, the *U. S. S. Nautilus*. The state's motto "He who transplanted still sustains" reflects its early history of early settlement. The name Connecticut is derived from the Indian word meaning "beside the long tidal river."

Delaware

The First State; Diamond State

The 18th. century, red-brick Colonial State House at Dover is the second oldest legislative house in the U.S. and has been the site of Delaware government since 1777. The State House was originally constructed to serve city, county, and state. Because of the lack of funds, construction took many years with 1791 the date when it was finished and could be used.

One of the dominant features of the interior is a free-standing, geometrically curved staircase. Rooms have been restored to the period 1792-1815, and give the Capitol the appearance of a museum. Delaware's governmental activity now is conducted in Legislative Hall, one of the first Georgian Revival buildings in America, built in 1933 and designed by E. William Martin. Today the Old State House remains officially Delaware's Capitol and contains the Governor's ceremonial office, and an 18th. century courtroom, legislative chamber and office. Restored in 1976, the Old State House can be seen as it was in 1793.

State History

The Dutch first settled Delaware in 1631 near the town of Lewes after the discovery of Delaware Bay by Henry Hudson in 1609. The Indians later destroyed the settlement. In 1638, settlers from Sweden established New Sweden, the first permanent settlement in Delaware and the present town of Wilmington. The Dutch, under Peter Stuyvesant returned in 1655 and took over the Delaware territory. Then in 1664, an English expedition seized New Amsterdam and took over Dutch Delaware for the Duke of York, who became James II. In 1682, he granted the family of William Penn a lease on Delaware. Although it was given a separate legislature in 1704, it remained under the jurisdiction of Pennsylvania until 1776.

During the Revolution only one battle was fought in the Delaware colony. Delaware was the first state to ratify the Constitution on December 7, 1787. During the Civil War most Delaware troops fought with the Union, but some from the southern part of the state that held slaves, fought with the Confederacy.

State Symbols

Delaware's state bird is the Blue Hen Chicken; its flower, the peach blossom; the state tree is the American Holly. Delaware's official beverage is milk; its fish, the weakfish. The lady bug is the official insect; sillimanite the state mineral. Its motto is "Liberty and Independence." The state is named after Thomas West, Lord De La Ware, the governor and captain general of Virginia.

Florida

The Sunshine State

The new, modern, gleaming white skyscraper building that is Florida's State Capitol in Tallahassee was dedicated in 1978 as a part of the Capitol Center. It is the fourth capitol building in Tallahassee.

In front of the new Capitol is the Old Capitol restored to its 1902 form and condition, the year the wings and the 136 foot high dome were added. A portion of it remains as the only carpenter built capitol in the United States. This third Capitol was begun in 1839 and completed in 1845 in the Tuscan Roman order with six stark modified Doric columns supporting a plain pedimened portico. The exterior is painted stucco over brick. The dome sets upon a square indented housing with two Ionic columns on each side. Classic urns adorn the corners. The traditional lantern housing is topped by a flag pole with the U. S. flag on it. Today the restored building houses a museum of Florida history.

State History

In 1513, Ponce de Leon was the first European to see Florida. He came again in 1521 to establish a colony but failed. In 1528, Panfilo de Narvaez explored the area and in 1539, Hernando de Soto arrived. In the next 300 years England, Spain, and France struggled for control of the territory. Spanish explorer, Pedro Menendez de Aviles, arrived in 1565 at St. Augustine and established the first permanent settlement in what is now the United States. Sir Francis Drake later burned the settlement.

Spain after years of struggle to establish colonies, ceded Florida to the British in 1763 in exchange for Havana, Cuba.

The area was returned to Spain in the Treaty of Paris (1783) that ended the American Revolution. During the War of 1812, Andrew Jackson invaded Spanish Florida and drove out the British at Pensacola. Finally in 1821, Spain ceded Spanish Florida to the U. S. Jackson became the first governor. The years prior to statehood were filled with the Second Seminol War (1835-42) in the attempts to drive out the Seminole Indians. Nearly four thousand Indians were sent to Oklahoma with about 300 escaping into the Everglades.

By 1840, attention turned to gaining statehood. Florida was admitted to the Union in March 3, 1845, as the 27th. state. Florida seceded from the Union and joined the Confederacy.in 1861. It was readmitted in 1868, although Federal troops occupied the state until 1877.

State Symbols

Florida's state bird is the mocking bird; its flower, the orange blossom; its tree is the sabal palmetto palm. Florida's official animal is the Florida panther; the freshwater fish, the largemouth bass; the saltwater fish the Atlantic sailfish. The state gem is the moonstone; its stone, the agatized coral. The saltwater mammal is the porpoise; the marine mammal, the mantee. The state motto is "In God We Trust." Florida is a name given by Ponce de Leon when he arrived during the Spanish Feast of Flowers or Pascua Florida.

Georgia

The Empire State of the South; The Peach State

Although the Georgia legislature had been meeting in Atlanta since 1868, the Classic Renaissance Capitol of Georgia located in Atlanta was not begun until 1884 and completed in 1889.

The Capitol is built primarily of Indiana oolitic limestone. Georgia marble is used on much of the interior of the building, but it proved too expensive to be used on the exterior. Its dome was gold-covered in 1959 and again in 1981. It measures seventy-five feet in diameter and reaches a height of 272 feet, 4 1/2 inches through the center. A fifteen foot high Greek-inspired female statue, holding a torch and a sword, representing freedom and commemorating the war dead, sets upon the domed lantern housing. The rotunda extends through from the second floor through the fourth floor to a height of 237 feet, 4 inches. The four-story front portico is supported by a colonnade of six Corinthian columns supporting a plain pediment with the state's seal engraved on it.

State History

Hernando de Soto was the first European to visit the area in 1540. By 1566, Spain had established Franciscan missions. Georgia was the last of the thirteen British colonies established on the seacoast when James

Edward Oglethorpe came to the Savannah area with 114 settlers on February 12, 1733, and a charter to establish a colony named after George II. By 1743, Oglethorpe surrendered his charter because of the dispute with Spain, and it became a British province.

During the Revolution, the settlers, many from the north, divided into two camps. Eventually the northern forces won and the Georgia delegation declared for independence and set up a revolutionary government with Savannah as the capital. Later it was moved to Augusta. Georgia was the fourth of the original thirteen colonies to ratify the Constitution, doing so on January 2, 1788.

The first permanent capital was built in Louisville in 1796. Then in 1804, a site on the Oconee River, was selected because it was nearer the population center. The new capital was named Milledgeville and served as the capital for sixty-one years. During the Civil War, Georgia seceded from the Union. Its land and its people were devastated by the war with much of the destruction occurring during General Sherman's march to the sea. Georgia's representatives reentered Congress in 1871. Following the war, the capital was moved to Atlanta.

State Symbols

Georgia's state flower is the Cherokee rose, a waxy white flower with a large golden center. The state bird is the brown thrasher, and the state tree is the live oak. Additional symbols of Georgia are the fish, largemouth bass; the game bird is the bobwhite quail; and the state insect, the honeybee. The state wildflower is the azalea; the state gem, quartz. The marine mammal is the Right whale. The official fossil is the shark tooth; the mineral is staurolite. Georgia's official song is Carmichael's "Georgia On My Mind." The state motto is "Wisdom, justice, and moderation."

Hawaii

The Aloha State

The very unique concrete and steel Capitol building for Hawaii is located in Honolulu on the island of Oahu, one of the eight islands of the state of Hawaii. The unusual Capitol building is highly symbolic. It is completely surrounded by an 80,000 square foot reflecting pool representing the Pacific Ocean that surrounds the Hawaiian Islands that form the state. The forty columns around the building rise to a crown of gentle curves representing the fronds of palm trees. These columns support a double roof that rises in a volcanic cone to a great open center representing a volcanic crater. The building's airy, open style is suitable for the gentle climate with its sun, rain, and trade winds. The entire building is constructed of a steel frame covered by a gray, poured concrete a reminder of the volcanic origin of the islands. Until the completion of the Capitol building, the Iolani Palace, meaning Bird of Heaven, served as the government building during Hawaii's republic, territorial, and early statehood periods.

State History

Hawaii was settled by the Polynesians from islands south of Hawaii about 700 A.D. Their first contact with European civilization occurred when Captain James Cook visited the islands in 1778. About the same time, King Kamehameha the Great started on a campaign to unite the islands under one government. Missionaries arrived in 1820, and by 1835 sugar production began. King Kamehameha III and his chiefs created the first constitution and legislature.

In 1893, with Queen Liliuokalani on the throne, Sanford Dole, leader of the Committee of Safety, declared the monarchy ended and a republic established. Hawaii was annexed by the U. S. in 1898 and a territory established. Sanford Dole served as the first governor from 1900-1903. Following World War II, the movement for statehood increased and on August 21, 1959, Hawaii became the 50th. state

State Symbols

Hawaii's flower is the hibiscus; its bird, the Hawaiian goose; its tree, the candlenut. Hawaii's motto is "The life of the land is perpetuated in righteousness." The state song is "Hawaiian Ponoi."

Idaho

The Gem State

The State Capitol building of Idaho is one of several state capitols patterned after the National Capitol in Washington, D. C. Idaho's Capitol located in Boise was begun in 1905 and completed in 1920, thirty years after Idaho became the 43rd. state.

The outside of the Capitol is built of Idaho limestone quarried at Table Rock. The Classical Renaissance dome is similar to the nation's Capitol and stands 208 feet high. The four large Corinthian columns at the entrance support a Classical Greek pediment. Facades with Ionic columns are on the two sides of the building to help visually to balance the structure. The drum of the classic dome is supported by Corinthian columns. On top of the lantern housing is a five foot, seven inch high solid copper eagle statue that was dipped in bronze and weighs 250 pounds.

While there are no marble columns within the building much of the interior is marble. The marble on the floors and staircases came from Alaska; the red-pink from Georgia; the blackish inlaid came from Italy; and the walls are Vermont marble. The interior columns around the rotunda are steel and are covered with a veneer surface called scagliola, which is a mixture of granite dust, gypsum, and glue.

State History

Lewis and Clark were the first to explore the area of Idaho in the fall of 1805 in their exploration of the area obtained in the Louisiana Purchase of 1803. Following their lead, British fur traders established outposts for the North West Company and the era of the mountain men began. By 1840, with the fur trade vanishing, the missionaries moved in to convert the Nez Perce Indians. Migration along the Oregon Trail brought more settlers.

In 1860, the Mormons established their first settlement at Franklin. That same year the Idaho gold rush occurred and more settlers arrived. The territory of Idaho was established and Lewiston became the territorial capital. In 1863, Boise was established as the permanent capital. At the same time that the railroads were being built in the 1880's, the Nez Perce Indian wars broke out in 1877-79, under the leadership of Chief Joseph. In 1889, territorial Governor Shoup called a state constitution convention and a constitution was adopted. Idaho became the 43rd. state on July 3, 1890.

State Symbols

Idaho's state flower is the springa; its bird, the mountain bluebird. The state tree is the Western white pine. The state gemstone is the star garnet. It is one of the few states to have a state horse, the Appaloosa. Idaho's state motto is "Let it be perpetual." The name Idaho comes from two Shoshone words: "Ed-dah-how" meaning "Behold, the sun is coming down the mountain;" and "Eda-hoe" meaning "The light is on the mountain."

Illinois

The Prairie State

Illinois' State Capitol building, overlooking the city of Springfield, is a large three-tiered structure topped with a dome that is 361 feet high. The building took 21 years to complete with construction begun in 1867, occupied in 1876, and completed in 1888.

Designed in the shape of a Latin cross, the Capitol is a fine example of Neoclassical Renaissance architecture with a front portico supported by delicate Corinthian columns. This order is also on the columns in the interior rotunda. The outer walls are limestone from Joliet and Lemont, Illinois. The north and east portico pillars are granite. The building's two wings are topped by mansard roofs. The interior marbles are domestic and imported but the rotunda walls and arches are of Missouri red granite. The third floor Corinthian columns are also Missouri red granite with blue granite and tuckahoe marble bases. The Corinthian columns support the inner dome with its striking artwork and stained-glass center skylight of the state seal. In the rotunda is the bronze statue "Illinois Welcoming the World," done for the Columbian Exposition in Chicago in 1893.

State History

While the fur traders were perhaps the first Europeans to visit Illinois, it was Pere Marquette and Joliet who officially are known to have explored the area and reached the site of Chicago in 1673. In 1679, La Salle descended the Illinois River and established a fort near today's Peoria. The British victory at Quebec in 1760 ended the French and Indian War with the French ceding the territory to the British in the Treaty of Paris in 1763. The British were then challenged by Chief Pontiac but his defeat came when he failed to capture Detroit. In 1778, American General George Rogers Clark captured the British fort at Kaskaskia and later Vincennes in 1779, thus bringing the area under United States control.

The area became a county of Virginia and settlers started to arrive. Illinois became part of the Northwest Territory in 1787 and a territory in 1809. In 1818 it attained statehood, entering the Union on December 3, 1818, as the 21st. state. However, peace did not come until after the defeat of Black Hawk in 1832 with the result of the removal of all Indians from Illinois by 1833.

The slavery issue was debated between Abraham Lincoln and Stephen Douglas in the senate race in 1858 which Douglas won. In 1860, the Republican party nominated Lincoln for president. During the Civil War, Illinois was pro-Union after sending Abraham Lincoln to the presidency.

State Symbols

Illinois' state bird is the cardinal, its flower is the butterfly violet. The state tree is the burr oak; the animal, the white-tailed deer. Its insect is the monarch butterfly; the state mineral is fluorite. The state motto is "State sovereignty, National union." The name Illinois comes from the Indian word and French suffix meaning "tribe of superior men."

A 68-foot-wide grand atruim with a double row of polished marble columns is the center of Indiana's Capitol.

Indiana

The Hoosier State

The ornate, Roman Renaissance, Corinthian styled Indiana State Capitol, located in the center of downtown Indianapolis, was completed in 1878, the second state capitol building in Indianapolis. Corydon was Indiana's first capital where a constitutional convention was held in 1816 when Indiana gained statehood. The first State House was constructed in

Indianapolis in the style of the Parthenon without the dome. The present Capitol building is constructed with mostly local materials, Indiana limestone, granite, and marble.

The Modern Renaissance, Neo-Roman designed building is topped by a 234 foot copper-covered solid stone dome atop which is the traditional small domed lantern housing. The east and south facades are adorned with Roman porticoes in the colonnades as well as flat pilasters in the Roman order. The pediment over the main entrance is supported by six Corinthian columns.

On the interior all corridors converge on the dome-covered rotunda where a forty-eight foot wide, stained glass inner dome rises 108 feet above the floor. A sixty-eight foot wide grand atrium, lined with marble columns and pilasters, extends the length of the building.

State History

The area of Indiana was originally inhabited by prehistoric Indian Moundbuilders that roamed the central United States. The first white men to enter the area were the French Jesuits. By the late 17th. and early 18th. centuries, French explorers, fur traders, and missionaries had arrived. Jacques Marquette arrived about 1675, followed by Robert Cavelier, Sieur de la Salle who explored the South Bend area between 1679-81. By 1731-32, a fort had been built at Vincennes. The 1763 Treaty of Paris gave the area to England and the area was transferred to the control in Quebec.

With the start of the Revolutionary War, Virginia dispatched George Rogers Clark to the Indiana area to secure it. He captured Vincennes from the British in 1779. In 1787, the federal government established the Northwest Territory and Vincennes became the capital of the Indiana Territory that included present Indiana, Illinois, Michigan, and Wisconsin. During the War of 1812 era, the final Indian uprising, led by Tecumseh and the Indian Confederation, was quelled by William Henry Harrison with his victory at Tippecanoe in 1811. Indiana's present boundaries were established when it became the 19th. state on December 11, 1816.

Although there was some opposition by Southern supporters during the Civil War, Indiana supported the Union,.

State Symbols

Indiana's state bird is the cardinal; its flower, the peony. The state tree is the tulip poplar; the state stone, Indiana limestone. The official state poem is "Indiana" by Arthur Franklin Mapes. Indiana's motto is "Crossroads of America."

Iowa

The Hawkeye State

The Iowa State Capitol overlooking Des Moines is one of the unique examples of 19th. century Neo-Romanesque architecture. The Romanesque styled Renaissance flavor of the building is brought about by the ornateness of its central gilded dome, highlighted by ornate bulls-eye windows with ornamentation on the top of each, and the rounded window lintels. Corinthian pilastered supports line the circumference of the tiers supporting the dome. A very ornate lantern housing tops the structure, 275 feet above the ground. Smaller ornate domes topped by lantern housings are on each corner of the capitol. The central portico with its decorated pediment is supported by six Corinthian columns.

This ornate building is the second capitol building in Des Moines and the sixth capitol in Iowa, the third since its becoming a state in 1846. It is built of a combination of limestone, sandstone, and granite from quarries in Iowa, Missouri, Illinois, Ohio, and Minnesota. The interior of the Capitol has twenty-nine varieties of marble on the floors, walls, and columns. Seven marble varieties are domestic and twenty-two are foreign. A mural over the grand stairway was done by Edwin Blashfield entitled "Westward." Another highlight are the six mosaics done by Frederick Dielman.

Originally, Iowa's capital was in Iowa City where it was moved from Burlington in 1841 while it was still the Iowa Territory. In 1857, the site of government was moved to a more central location in Des Moines. The Old Brick Capitol served as a capitol until 1892 when it was destroyed by fire. The present Capitol building had been under construction since 1871, but delays prevented its completion until 1886. Even then the interior was not completed until after the Old Brick Capitol burned.

State History

Until 1673, when Pere Marquette and Louis Joliet explored the area for France, Iowa was inhabited by the Moundbuilders. While France claimed the area, they ceded the part west of the Mississippi to Spain in 1762. The first permanent settlement was by the French-Canadian, Julien Dubuque, in 1788.

The area was not explored until after the Louisiana Purchase in 1803 when Lewis and Clark moved through the area. Soon settlements of farmers crossed the Mississippi River and moved into the area, and after passing through many territorial changes when the area was a part of Louisiana, then Michigan, and finally, Wisconsin, the Territory of Iowa was established. By the mid-1840's, the Indians in the territory had signed over the lands and by 1846, Iowa was ready for statehood. It became the 29th. state on December 28, 1846. During the Civil War, Iowa strongly supported the Union cause, sending 80,000 troops to the Union army.

State Symbols

Iowa's state flower is the wild rose; its bird, the Easter goldfinch. The state tree is the oak. The state rock is geode. Iowa's motto is "Our liberties we prize and our rights we will maintain." Iowa's name is derived from the Indian word meaning "this is the place" or "beautiful land.

Iowa's original Capitol is on the University of Iowa's campus in Iowa City.

Kansas
The Sunflower State

The magnificent domed Capitol building of Kansas is located on a sixteen acre grounds in Topeka. In 1861, an election was held where to locate the capital, and Topeka won over Lawrence and Fort Leavenworth where the territorial capital had been located. Construction of the domed building using Kansas limestone was begun in the late 1800's and completed in March, 1903.

The Classical French Renaissance Capitol is a fine example of the Corinthian styled architecture with six Corinthian columns supporting a plain pediment at the front. Secondary pediments on each side are supported by pilasters with Corinthian capitals. The green copper dome rises 304 feet from the ground to the top of the lantern housing and is supported by a three-tierd double octagonal base. The interior floors and wainscoting are primarily Georgian marble with some Tennessee marble and foreign marbles used as well. The Capitol is noted also for the dramatic Kansas history murals of John Steuart Curry that depict Kansas history and people. The most famous is the dramatic larger than life mural of John Brown with a Bible in his upraised left hand and in his right, a rifle. "Burning Kansas" with free soil and proslavery forces are pictured behind Brown.

State History

The first known European visitor to Kansas area was Francisco Coronado in 1541. Other fur traders traversed the region for the next two centuries. It wasn't until after the Louisiana Purchase in 1803, that the area was again explored. Meriwether Lewis and William Clark came in 1804, Zebulon Pike in 1806, and in 1819, Stephen Long explored and labeled the area the "Great American Desert" on maps.

Kansas became the starting point for many of the pioneers who traveled westward. The Oregon Trail passed through the northern part of the area. Although the Missouri Compromise made it a 'free-soil' area, conflict over slavery reached a peak when the Kansas-Nebraska Act, which created the territory in 1854, left the question up to the residents. The conflict culminated in 1856, when John Brown and his sons murdered five men. By 1859 the anti-slavery group had won and adopted a constitution that forbad slavery. Kansas became the 34th. state on January 29, 1861, just as the Civil War started. Because of the proximity to the war and the violence brought about whether Kansas would be a slave or free state, Kansas was called 'Bleeding Kansas.' Following the Civil War and the building of the railroad, Kansas became the center of the great cattle drives and the old West image of the cattle towns of Abilene, Dodge City, and Wichita was established.

State Symbols

Kansas' state flower is the native sunflower; its bird, the Western meadowlark. The state animal is the American buffalo; its insect, the honeybee. The state tree is the cottonwood. The state song "Home on the Range." Kansas' state motto is "To the stars through difficulties."

Kentucky

The Bluegrass State

The state of Kentucky's huge, multi-columned Capitol building sets on a low hill overlooking the city of Frankfort, set in a picturesque valley formed by the Kentucky River. Even though Kentucky became a state in 1792, the present Capitol was not built and used until 1910. Until then the Old Capitol was the center of Kentucky government.

Kentucky's Capitol is surrounded by an architectural stone terrace which supports seventy monolithic columns. The building's exterior is faced with oolitic Indiana limestone above a base of Vermont marble. The marble used inside the Capitol is from Georgia. Architect Frank Mills

Andrew designed the rotunda, dome, and lantern after that of the Chapel of the Invalides in Paris. The dome is 212 feet high from ground level. The drum that supports the dome is supported by a colonnade of paired Ionic columns. A balustrade runs around the dome's base. The front portico Ionic columns support a pediment with allegorical figures representing Kentucky's progress.

An interior reception room is furnished after the period of Louis XIV, based on Marie Antoinette's drawing room in the Grand Trionon at Versailles. The stairs, balustrades, and bannisters imitate the Paris Opera. The most impressive interior feature is the 403 foot long nave or transverse axis of the rotunda which is lined with thirty-six Ionic columns of pale gray scagliola, imitating ornamental marble.

State History

After the Moundbuilders disappeared from along the Ohio River, the Shawnee and Cherokee Indians lived in the area that became Kentucky. The Appalachian Mountains proved a challenge to anyone wanting to move westward and it wasn't until 1750 when Dr. Thomas Walker discovered the Cumberland Gap that there was a hope to move westward. Finally in 1769, Daniel Boone and John Finley led a group of settlers through the Gap and settlements were established along the Wilderness Road or Boone's Trace. Harrodsburg became the first permanent settlement in 1774.

During the Revolution and until 1782, British inspired Indian raids and Virginia and North Carolina, vying for the claim to the area, kept further settlement down. Eventually, Kentucky became a part of Virginia, but by 1790, the frontiersmen had started a separation movement, and asked Congress for admittance as a separate state. It was admitted to the Union on June 1, 1792, as the 15th. state.

During the Civil War, Kentucky never left the Union, but divided sentiments saw the state sending troops to both sides. Both President Lincoln and Jefferson Davis, President of the Confederacy, were born in Kentucky. Frankfort was the only state capital captured by the Confederacy.

State Symbols

The Kentucky state flower is the goldenrod; its bird, the cardinal. The state tree is the Kentucky coffee tree; the game animal, the gray squirrel. Kentucky's state motto is "United we stand, divided we fall." The name Kentucky is from a Cherokee word for "prairie" or " barren ground."

Louisiana

The Pelican State

Louisiana's towering State Capitol building at Baton Rouge, which became capital after the Civil War, is the tallest capitol in the United States and was the first domeless 20th. century capitol building built in the U. S. Dreyfous, one of the designers, called it Modern Classic design.

The modern skyscraper structure, located on the banks of the Mississippi River, rises 34 stories, 450 feet above the city. The granite and marble building, completed in 1932, was constructed during the governorship of Huey P. Long, Louisiana's flamboyant and controversial politician. Later as Senator, Long was assassinated in the corridor of the Capitol building he had built. Even though it is not of the traditional styled domed capitol building, it still has the traditional lantern housing topping off the multi-tiered building top.

The facade of the building is finished with Alabama limestone. Its interior is Art Deco, finished in rich colored marble panels on the walls and floors. The impressive, 120 foot long Memorial Hall has a floor of polished lava from Mt. Vesuvius. The center of the floor has a large bronze plaque with a relief map of Louisiana.

State History

Louisiana has a long history going back to the early explorations by Spanish explorers as early as 1530 when Cabeza de Vaca and Panifilo de Narvaez visited the area. In 1541, Hernando de Soto claimed the northern part of Louisiana for Spain, one of ten flags to fly over the state during its history. The first permanent settlement was by the French in 1714 at Natchitoches. Later in 1723, they founded New Orleans. France ceded the area to Spain in 1762, took it back in 1800, and finally sold it to the United States in 1803 as part of the Louisiana Purchase, thus giving the new nation control of the Mississippi River.

The French influence was strengthened when French-Canadians or "Cajuns" arrived following the end of the French and Indian War when they were exiled from Canada. Although the Treaty of Ghent ended the War of 1812, news was late in reaching the U. S. and forces led by Andrew Jackson defeated the British in the Battle of New Orleans, the final battle in the War of 1812. Louisiana was given statehood on April 30, 1812, as the 18th. state in the United States and the first state to be established from the Louisiana Purchase. Louisiana seceded from the Union on January 21, 1861. New Orleans was captured by the Union by David Farragut and it remained in the Union hands for the entire war while the western portion of the state remained under Confederate influence.

State Symbols

Louisiana's state bird is the Eastern brown pelican; the state flower, the magnolia. Its state tree is the bald cypress. The state dog is the Louisiana Catahoula leopard dog; the reptile is the alligator. The state gem is the agate; the insect, the honeybee. Milk is the official drink. The state crustacean is the crawfish; the fossil, petrified palmwood. Louisiana's motto is "Union, justice, and confidence." The state song is "Give Me Louisiana." The state was named by La Salle for Louis XIV of France and the King's mother, Anna.

Maine

The Pine Tree State

The majestic pale-gray, Maine granite Greek Revival State House of Maine is located in Augusta and situated on the banks of the Kennebec River. The center section of the domed building embodies the strong architectural style of its designer, Charles Bulfinch. The Capitol building's design was Bulfinch's last major architectural project in which he preserved the general outline of the Boston State House, another of his projects, but the design gave the Maine Capitol an air of simplicity rather than an exact copy. The State House was started in 1829; completed in 1831.

When it was remodeled in 1910, the high dome and rotunda were added thus changing the original Bulfinch design with only the front Doric columns over the arches portion remaining of the original Bulfinch structure. The upper front portico with Doric columns is a copy of the Temple of Vesta in Rome. Doric columns support the drum of the 185 foot dome with an exterior balcony with a granite balustrade encircling the dome. On the top of the lantern housing is W. Clark Noble's copper gold-covered figure of Wisdom.

State History

Maine's rocky coast was explored by the English Cabots in 1498-99. Over 100 years later the French arrived. It was the English who settled on the Kennebec River in 1607 under the leadership of George Weymouth. John Smith from the early Jamestown settlement explored the area in 1614. It became a part of Massachusetts in 1691 and remained a part of that state until 1820 when it attained statehood.

The British remained in control of the area until the Revolution. During the war for freedom from England, Maine sent many regiments against the British. Valley Forge, Bunker Hill, and the siege of Boston saw Maine volunteers fighting the British. In turn, British raids on the coastal settlements caused much suffering. Portland was burned during the War.

The Treaty of Ghent in 1814 following the War of 1812, settled most of the state's boundaries, but the northern one remained in dispute until after the bloodless Aroostook War in 1842. Originally Portland was the capital following Maine's separation from Massachusetts in 1819, when on March 15, 1820, it became the 23rd. state in the Union. After a search for a permanent capital, Augusta was chosen by the legislature and became the state's capital in 1827. During the Civil War, Maine sent thousands of men to fight on the Union side, leaving the state depleted of men and money.

State Symbols

Maine's state flower is the white pine cone and tassel. Its state bird, the chickadee. The state tree is the Eastern white pine. Its wild animal is the moose; the domesticated animal, the Maine coon cat. The state fish is the landlocked salmon; its insect, the honeybee. Maine's mineral is tourmaline; its fossil, *pertica quadrifarta*. Maine's motto is "I direct;" its state song is "State of Maine Song." The states's name is said to have originated from its maritime location when its land form was referred to as "the Main" to distinguish it from the many coastal islands.

Maryland

The Old Line State

Maryland's Colonial State House facing Annapolis Harbor in Annapolis was completed in the years 1772-1779 and remains today the oldest such structure in the United States in daily use as a legislative building. It is the only state capitol building to serve as the nation's capitol, serving as the peacetime capitol from November, 1783 to August, 1784. While it was begun in 1772, its completion was delayed by the American Revolution.

The present dome, the largest wooden dome in the U. S., replaced an earlier built cupola in 1788. The dome is constructed of cypress beams and held together by wooden pegs. The earlier portion of the Capitol is built of wood and plaster, but the newer parts have matched Italian Carrara marble walls and columns which were added between 1902-05. In the old Senate Chamber is Charles Willson Peal's painting of Washington, Lafayette, and Tilghman at Yorktown.

Notable events that occurred in the Maryland State House were the meeting of the Continental Congress in the years between 1783-84, George Washington resigning as Commander-in-Chief of the Continental Army in December, 1783, and it was in the same room less than a month later that the Treaty of Paris was ratified in January, 1784, thus ending the Revolutionary War.

State History

Spanish explorers were credited with visiting the area of Maryland as early as 1570. Later, Maryland was explored by Captain John Smith in 1608 when he sailed up the Potomac River and sailed up Chesapeake Bay. In 1632, Great Britain gave a land grant to Cecil Calvert, Lord Baltimore, and in 1634, he established a settlement for Catholics to escape persecution in England.

The state's nickname "Old Line" came from the Battle of Long Island during the Revolution when brave Maryland troops battled and held off British regulars. In the War of 1812, the state was invaded by the British, and when a British fleet tried to take Fort McHenry in 1814, Francis Scott Key wrote the "Star Spangled Banner."

Union forces occupied Maryland during the Civil War and the bloodiest battle of the war, Antietam, took place in Maryland. Of the thirteen original colonies, Maryland became the seventh state to vote for ratification on April 28, 1788.

State Symbols

Maryland's state bird is the Baltimore oriole; its flower, the black-eyed susan. The state tree is the white oak; the insect is the Baltimore checkerspot butterfly, The fish is the striped bass; the fossil shell, *ecphora quadricostata*. "Maryland, My Maryland" is the state song. The motto "Manly deeds, womanly words" shows a balanced life approach. Maryland was named in honor of Queen Henrietta Maria, wife of Charles I of England.

Massachusetts

The Bay State

The Massachusetts State House overlooking Boston Common is noted for its gold dome and red brick front, all that remain of the Bulfinch designed building that was completed on January 11, 1798. The State House is the oldest building on Beacon Hill in Boston. Originally the wooden dome was coppered by Paul Revere in 1802. It wasn't until 1872 that the gilded gold was added.

Besides the thirty-five foot gold dome, a dominant feature of the State House is the first floor arcade with a Corinthian columned porch over it. The original portion of the Capitol building was constructed of Maine wood. The pine cone on the top of the lantern housing on the dome symbolizes the importance of the lumber industry in early New England economy. On the interior, Doric Hall is the most striking with its ten Doric columns and collection of paintings, statuary, and cannon. The original columns were carved pine logs, but the present copies are made from iron and plaster.

State History

The coastal area of Massachusetts was first explored by the English explorer, John Cabot in 1497. His exploration became the basis for England's claim to North America. The first settlement was by the Pilgrims in 1620 at Plymouth. They established an autocratic theocracy that showed no tolerance for other religions. In 1675-76, a bloody Indian uprising, King Philip's War against the encroachment of the white man spread across New England.

At first, Massachusetts settlers had almost total freedom from England, but by the late 1700's, the English monarchs made it a royal colony under a governor. By 1760's with the enactment of the Sugar Act (1764), the Stamp Act (1765), and the Tea Tax (1773), the state became the center of the American Revolutionary spirit. Events such as the "Boston Massacre" (1770) and the Boston Tea Party (1773) in which taxed tea was thrown into Boston Harbor, set the stage for the American Revolution.

The first battle of the Revolution took place in Lexington on April 17, 1775. It was the sixth state of the original thirteen colonies to ratify the Constitution on February 6, 1778. In 1780, Massachusetts ratified its state constitution. It is the only state still governed under its original constitution, which became the model for the Bill of Rights of the United States Constitution. The state became a center for the abolitionist movement and during the Civil War, sent over 150,000 men to fight for the Union cause.

State Symbols

The Massachusetts state flower is the Mayflower; its tree the American elm. The state bird is the chickadee; its fish, the cod. Its dog is the Boston terrier; the horse, the Morgan horse. The state insect is the ladybug; the marine mammal, the right whale. Its mineral is babingtnite; its fossil, Dinosaur track. The state's historical rock is Plymouth rock; its explorer rock, dighton rock. The state gem is rhodonite; the rock is Roxbury pudding stone. Building stone is granite. The state beverage is cranberry juice. The state poem is "Blue Hills of Massachusetts" by Katherine E. Mullen. Massachusetts' motto is "By the sword she seeks peace, but peace only under liberty." The state is named after a tribe of Indians who lived in the area of the Great Blue Hill, south of Boston. Massachusetts means "at or about the great hill."

Michigan

The Great Lake State; Wolverine State

The state's capital was moved from Detroit to Lansing in 1847 and is the third capitol in the state's history. The Lansing Capitol, built from 1873-1878, is patterned after the Nation's Capitol and was designed by Elijah Meyers, the architect who designed the Texas and Colorado Capitols.

The Classical Renaissance structure is based upon the cruciform church plan with the high central dome rising 255 feet, 6 inches above the ground at the intersect of the cross; 276 feet to the top of the lantern housing. The main facade is the eastern entrance with its design

66

emphasis, a huge Massachusetts granite stair and three doors. Michigan's progress is depicted in allegorical base relief on the entablature in the pediment above the entrance. The three main floors are treated with pilastered Orders in ascending order. First floor columns are of the Tuscan order; the second floor, Ionic; and the third floor, Corinthian. The building's foundation is limestone from Lamont, Illinois, with the rest of the granite building faced with white Ohio sandstone. Rails, decorative urns and pedestals are of Joliet, Illinois, limestone. The octagonal high dome is of cast iron and covered with sheet metal painted white and is topped by an octagonal-shaped lantern housing. It is supported by a Ionic colonnade with each quarter having a small portico.

The Capitol's interior is a showplace of the decorative arts with the House and Senate ceilings made up of glass squares showing the states' seals. The rotunda features a leaded thick glass floor with 976 panels and rises four floors to its center blue focal point. Viewed from above, the floor appears to be bowl shaped.

State History

In 1618, French fur traders and missionaries came to the Michigan area. That year Etienne Brule was the first European to explore the area at Saulte Ste. Marie. Jean Nicolet came to the area in 1634. Later in 1668, the Jesuit, Father Jacques Marquette set up a Jesuit mission at Sault Ste. Marie. Later Fort Michilimackinac was built at the Straits and by 1701, Detroit was established. The Michigan area was under French control until 1763 when it became a British territory with the signing of the Paris Treaty ending the French and Indian War.

The Treaty of Paris of 1783 ending the American Revolution made it officially a part of the United States, but it wasn't until Anthony Wayne defeated the British Indian allies at Fallen Timbers, Ohio, in 1794, and in 1796, occupied Detroit, that the area was stabilized as United States territory. The area was part of the Old Northwest Territory until 1800, when it became part of the Indiana Territory until 1805. Michigan was finally freed of the British during the War of 1812 when Oliver Perry's Lake Erie victory and William H. Harrison's forces drove the British back into Canada in 1813. It became the Michigan Territory from 1805 until 1837 when Michigan entered the Union on January 26, 1837, as the 26th. state.

State Symbols

Michigan's state bird is the robin. Its flower is the apple blossom; its tree, the white pine. The state fish is the trout. Michigan's gem is the greenstone; its stone, Petroskey stone. The state song is "Michigan, My Michigan;" the state's motto is "If you seek a pleasant peninsula, look about you." Michigan's name comes from the Ojibwa tribal word "missikamaa" meaning "it is a big lake."

Minnesota

The North Star State, The Gopher State

Minnesota's Roman Renaissance styled Capitol building in St. Paul is the third structure to serve as the state capitol. The first was built in 1854, the second in 1882. The present Capitol building was begun in 1896 and completed in 1905.

The steps, balustrades, foundation, and terraces are constructed of gray granite from St. Cloud, Minnesota. The exterior walls and dome are made of Georgian marble. Above the main entrance to the capitol are six statues by Daniel Chester French representing virtues: Wisdom, courage, Bounty, Truth, Integrity, and Prudence. At the base of the dome is another sculpture group by French and Edward Potter, a steel and copper, gold-leafed covered group entitled "The Progress of the State." The charioteer represents prosperity by holding a horn of plenty filled with Minnesota products and a banner with "Minnesota."

The dome with bulls-eye windows and elaborate paired Corinthian columns supporting narrow porticoes encircling the dome's base. It is topped with a gold-covered ball on a columned lantern housing 223 feet above the ground. Hanging from the inner rotunda is an Austrian crystal chandelier with 95 light bulbs that are lighted on special state occasions.

State History

In the 17th. century Minnesota territory was first visited by fur traders and missionaries. Two Frenchmen, Pierre Radisson and Sieur des Groseilliers, are believed to have visited the area in the mid-1660's, but even well into the 18th. century, it was the domain of the Chippewa and Sioux Indians. Father Louis Hennepin, who explored the upper Mississippi in 1680, recorded the site of the future Minneapolis.

In 1763, Britain made the area a part of the their claim to all land east of the Mississippi following the French and Indian War. After the American Revolution, the U. S. took over the area in the Treaty of Paris of 1783, ending the Revolutionary War, and then in 1803, the U. S. received the western portion as part of the Louisiana Purchase. Zebulon Pike purchased lands from the Indians in 1805, on which Fort Snelling was built in 1819. Treaties were made with the Sioux and the Chippewa and a more intense influx of settlers occurred. After an Indian uprising in 1862, the government drove the Indians from the state. With the increased population, a constitutional convention was held in 1857, and Minnesota entered the Union on May 11, 1858 as the 32nd. state.

With the increase of commerce, Minneapolis and St. Paul grew up as the Twin Cities on the banks of the Mississippi. When the Civil War began, Minnesota was the first state to offer Federal troops.

State Symbols

Minnesota's state bird is the loon. Its state flower is the pink and white lady's slipper or moccasin flower. The state tree is the Norway pine; the state mushroom, the morel. The official state grain is wild rice; its gem, Lake Superior agate. The official drink is milk; the official fish is walleye. Minnesota's song is "Hail, Minnesota." The state motto is "The star of the North." The name Minnesota comes from the two Sioux Indian words meaning "sky-tinted water."

Mississippi

The Magnolia State

The Greek Renaissance styled Mississippi State Capitol set on a terrace in downtown Jackson was begun in 1901 and completed in 1903. The building was the first all-electric building in Jackson, replacing the first Capitol completed in 1850, which today is a historic museum.

The Capitol is constructed of Bedford limestone with a base of Georgia granite. The structure's lofty entrance portico has six Corinthian columns supporting the classical pediment with the entablature containing figures representing the arts, resources, and industries of Mississippi. Corinthian columns support the drum of the dome that rises 180 feet above the entrance. It is fashioned after the Nation's Capitol and is topped by a fifteen foot wing-span copper eagle in flight that is covered with gold leaf. The building's two wings are semi-circular Corinthian colonnades supporting saucer domes which lend a greater majesty and gracefulness to the traditional classical architecture of the capitol building.

The interior features striking blue Vermont marble on a base of Black Belgium marble. The rotunda has Italian marble trimmed with jet black New York marble. The friezes and columns are of scagliola.

State History

The Mississippi territory was explored by Hernando De Soto who claimed the area for Spain as early as 1541, the year in which he discovered the Mississippi River. Father Marquette explored the region in 1673. Later LaSalle's explorations took him the length of the Mississippi, and in 1682, France used his explorations to claim the territory.

In 1763, at the Treaty of Paris, which ended the French and Indian War, Britain claimed all the area except for Louisiana which went to Spain. It was during and after the American Revolution that the entire area was in contention between England, France, and the U. S. Spain occupied the area during the Revolution but ceded the territory to the U. S. in 1795.

It was the Louisiana Purchase in 1803, that gave the Mississippi River valley to the U. S. Mississippi became the 20th. state to enter the Union on December 10, 1817.

In 1861, Mississippi was the second state to secede from the Union and was the site for intense fighting. The culmination of the fighting occurred at Vicksburg when General Grant defeated the Confederate forces for control of the lower Mississippi in 1863.

State Symbols

Mississippi's state bird is the mockingbird; its flower, the magnolia. The state tree is the magnolia; the insect is the honeybee. The state fish is the largemouth bass; the marine mammal, the bottlenosed dolphin. The land mammal is the white-tailed deer. The state fossil is the prehistoric whale; its shell, the oyster shell. The state drink is milk. The state song is "Go, Mississippi;" the state motto is "By valor and arms." The word "Mississippi" comes from "misi sipi," an Oibway Indian word meaning "great water."

Missouri

The Show Me State

The magnificent Roman Renaissance style State Capitol building in Jefferson City, completed between 1913 and 1917, after the second capitol building was struck by lightning and burned in 1911, is located on a limestone bluff on the south bank of the Missouri River.

The Capitol's exterior and much of the interior is finished in Carthage limestone marble, a stone native to southwest Missouri. The same limestone is used on the interior floors and the rotunda while a warm grey Phoenix marble cover the interior walls. There are 134 columns inside the building to go along with the many Corinthian columns that surround the building's exterior. Corinthian columns support a front portico with a decorated pediment in its entablature. The classic dome supported by paired Corinthian columns is 238 feet above the ground. Atop the lantern on the dome at a height of 262 feet is the classic bronze figure of Ceres, goddess of grain and agriculture by Sherry Fry.

The thirteen by eighteen foot bronze front doors are,-the largest cast since the Roman era. An outstanding interior feature is the thirty foot wide grand stairway. In the rotunda, hanging from the dome's eye, 170 feet above, is a 9000 pound bronze chandelier. The House lounge is the most striking room. It contains murals by Thomas Hart Benton entitled "A Social History of the State of Missouri."

State History

Missouri's early history includes explorations by Hernando de Soto in 1541. Later Frenchmen Father Jacques Marquette and Louis Joliet descended the Mississippi River and explored the Missouri area in 1673. La Salle claimed the area for France in 1682. The first European settlement was a mission at the site of St. Louis in 1700 which became a fur trading post in 1764. French hunters and lead miners made the first permanent settlement in 1735 at Ste. Genevieve.

The territory was ceded to Spain in 1763, and later was part of the Louisiana Purchase sold to the U. S. by Napoleon in 1803 for $15 million. Missouri was organized as a territory in 1812, and became the 24th. state of the Union on August 10, 1821, as a part of the Missouri Compromise that admitted it as a slave state and Maine as a free state. During the Civil War, forces on both sides made Missouri a divided state although officially it remained on the Union side but contributed men to both Union and Confederate forces.

State Symbols

Missouri's state bird is the bluebird; its flower, the hawthorn. The state tree is the flowering dogwood; the state insect, the honey bee. Missouri's state song is "The Missouri Waltz;" the state musical instrument, the fiddle. The state rock is the mozarkite; the state mineral, galena, the bearer of lead ore. Missouri's state motto is "The welfare of the people shall be the supreme law." The state is named after a Sioux Indian tribe. Missouri is said to mean "town of large canoes," "wooden canoe people," or "he of the big canoe."

Montana

The Treasure State

The Montana State Capitol at Helena is situated on a hill overlooking the Helena Valley, which Lewis and Clark named the "Prickly Pear Valley" in 1805. The Capitol building, of a traditional Neoclassical Greek Ionic design, was dedicated in 1902 after four years of construction. Helena had served as the territorial capital until 1889 when it became the state capital.

The spartan appearing Capitol is faced with sandstone from a Columbus, Montana, quarry. The two wings of the Capitol were added a decade later and was constructed of Jefferson county granite to match the earlier sandstone. The copper-sheathed dome is topped by a statue of Liberty, symbolic of Helena being chosen as the states's capital over its rival, Anaconda. It stands 165 feet above ground level. The Capitol's interior is done in French Renaissance fashion and features a rotunda surrounded by Ionic columns. The interior dome rises 100 feet above the rotunda's terrazzo floor encasing the Great Seal of Montana. A barrel vault skylight illuminates the flaring grand staircase of white marble and brass decorations. In the House of Representative Chamber is Charles M. Russell's painting of Lewis and Clark meeting the Indians at Ross' Hole in 1805. Above the grand staircase a mural shows the driving of the golden spike commemorating the railroads coming to Montana.

State History

Montana was first explored by the French in 1742. A portion of the state was part of the Louisiana Purchase in 1803, and later the explorations of Lewis and Clark in 1805-06 added more territory to the area that would become Montana in 1889. Fur trade and missionary work brought civilization to the territory which was racked by Indian uprisings in the mid-1800's. Gold was discovered at Gold Creek in 1852, but it wasn't until 1862, that the big gold find occurred and the rush was on.

Helena sprung up at the location of the Last Chance Gulch placer mine. With more settlers entering the area, lawlessness reigned. Eventually, concerned inhabitants took the law into their own hands and drove the outlaws from the territory. Because of broken treaties by the white man, the Indian wars became more intense. They were culminated by the Battle of the Little Big Horn in 1876. Finally, with the building of the Northern Pacific Railway in 1883, population accelerated and the Montana territory established. On November 8, 1889, Montana became the 41st. state.

State Symbols

Montana's flower is the bitterroot; its state bird is the Western meadowlark. The state tree is the Ponderosa pine; the animal, the grizzly bear. The blackspotted cutthroat trout is the state fish. The state gems are the sapphire and Montana agate; the state grass, bluebunch grass. Montana's state song is "Montana." Its motto is "Gold and Silver." Montana is a Spanish word for "mountain."

Nebraska

The Cornhusker State

The white, 400 foot imposing skyscraper Capitol building of Nebraska can be seen for miles across the flat plain in approaching the capital city of Lincoln. The present building is the third capitol for the state. The towering Art Deco Capitol building was constructed around the second capitol while it was being used. Construction was begun in 1922, with the old capitol razed in 1925, and the tower begun. It was completed in 1930, with the entire project completed in 1932, the 65th. year of statehood. The Capitol building is ranked by the American Institute of Architects as the fourth modern architectural wonder along with the Taj Mahal and England's Parliament building.

The four-tierd, gold-domed "Tower on the Plains" is topped by the nineteen foot statue of "The Sower," her arm flung out, broadcasting grain, the chief product of the state. The Great Hall that connects the vestibule to the rotunda features a floor mosaic made up of white and black Belgium marble depicting the Spirits of the Soil, Vegetation, and Animal Life. Colorful mosaics depicting nature's gifts to the inhabitants of the plains cover the vestibule ceiling. The gleaming white limestone exterior has many artistic features from a base relief of the Mayflower Compact signing to the Gettysburg Address behind a Daniel French sculpture of Lincoln. The Capitol building houses the only state unicameral legislature in the United States.

State History

The area that became the state of Nebraska was first explored by Spanish and French explorers and fur traders in the years before the Louisiana Purchase in 1803. In 1714, Etienne de Bourgmond, a French explorer, traveled the Missouri River to the Platte. In a treaty separate from the 1763 Treaty of Paris ending the French and Indian War, Spain gained control of the area west of the Mississippi.

Acquired by the United States in the Louisiana Purchase in 1803, Lewis and Clark came through the area in 1804-05. Other explorers were Zebulon Pike in 1806, Stephen Long in 1819-20, Henry Dodge in 1835, John Fremont, 1842-1844, and G. Warren in 1855-1857. The first permanent settlement was at Bellevue, near Omaha, in 1823.

By 1854, there were enough settlers and the area was of such strategic value for building the transcontinental railroad that it came under the Kansas-Nebraska Act that allowed the residents to determine if the territory would be a slave or free state. It was the Homestead Act of 1862, that brought more settlers. Because of this increase in population, Nebraska entered the Union on March 1, 1867, as the 37th. state.

State Symbols

The state flower is the golden rod; the state bird, the Western meadowlark. The cottonwood tree is the state tree; the grass is little blue stem grass. Its insect is the honeybee; the state mammal, the white-tailed deer. The state gem is the blue agate; the rock, the prairie agate. The state fossil is the mammoth. Nebraska's state song is "Beautiful Nebraska;" its motto, "Equality before the law." The word Nebraska comes from the Osage Indian word "nebraska" meaning" flat water."

Nevada

The Sagebrush State; Silver State

The tan sandstone Capitol building of Nevada is located in Carson City, named after the Western frontiersman, Kit Carson. The bill to construct the capitol building was signed on February 23, 1869. The building was completed in 1870-1 with the sandstone for the structure quarried at the Nevada State Prison quarry outside of Carson City.

The two story Capitol, built in the form of a Grecian cross, is topped by six-sided silver-covered elliptical dome. The architecture of the structure is a compound of the Greek orders, Doric, Ionic, and Corinthian. Each of the entrances has a portico supported by Doric columns with the east and west entrances having four. The original Supreme Court room has a formal Greek styled backdrop with Ionic pilasters. The cupola, rising 48 feet above the roof, 120 feet above the ground, is octagonal in form, 83 feet in diameter and is supported by sixteen ornamental pilasters and buttresses with windows between the columns with Corinthian caps. Inside the Capitol, a 400 foot ornamental frieze painted in 1917, runs around the walls and depicts Nevada's industry and resources. Ornate ceilings hold chandeliers and the double-arched windows have panes of twenty-six ounce French Crystal. The wainscotting, arches, and floors are of Alaskan marble.

State History

Nevada was first explored by the Spanish with the first record of a European that of a monk, Francisco Garces, in 1776. Later Hudson Bay Company fur trappers led by Peter Ogden explored the north and central portions of the area and discovered the Humboldt River in 1825. In 1826-27, fur trader, Jedediah Smith, crossed the state. Finally, in the years 1843-1845, Captain John Fremont explored the entire area and created interest in the area. In 1848, the U. S. acquired the area as part of the settlement of the Mexican War in the Treaty of Guadalupe-Hidalgo. By 1849, the first permanent settlement was established at Mormon Station, now Genoa. At one time the area was a part of the territory of Utah and of New Mexico. Nevada received territorial status on March 2, 1861.

During the Civil War, Nevada remained loyal to the Union cause, providing gold and silver. After a constitutional convention drafted a constitution in Carson City which was later ratified, Lincoln proclaimed Nevada a part of the Union on October 31, 1864, as the 36th. state.

State Symbols

Nevada's state flower is the sagebrush; its bird, the mountain bluebird. The state tree is the single-leaf pinon. The state animal is the Desert Bighorn sheep; the state fish, the Lohonton cutthroat trout. Nevada's fossil is ichthyosaur; its metal, silver. The official grass is Indian rice grass. The state song is "Home Means Nevada;" its motto "All for Our Country." The name Nevada come from a Spanish word meaning "snow covered."

New Hampshire

The Granite State

The oldest State House in the U. S. with the legislature still meeting in it is the State House of New Hampshire located in Concord, site of New Hampshire's first legislative session in 1782. The State House has been enlarged several times because the New Hampshire legislature is the largest legislative body in the U. S. There may be as many as four hundred members attending a single session. They are elected in the towns and city wards to serve as representatives. The state senate has twenty-four members.

The cornerstone of the Neoclassic structure was not laid until 1816, and the building, constructed of local Concord granite and Vermont marble, was completed in 1819. The building's dominant feature is the double portico with the lower floor entrance Doric columns supporting the upper portico that in turn supports the classic Roman pediment using Corinthian columns. A balustrade encircles the flat roof. Its bullseye windowed gold dome is topped by a lantern housing on which is a golden eagle with wings poised for flight. The present eagle statue is a replacement for the first statue taken down in 1957. Inside the Senate rooms are the murals of Barry Faulkner depicting events in New Hampshire history.

State History

The first explorers to visit New Hampshire were Englishmen, Martin Pring in 1603, and Samuel de Champlain in 1605 and Captain John Smith in 1614. The first settlement was at Little Harbor, near Rye and Portsmouth, in 1623. In 1629, the name New Hampshire, after Hampshire, England, was given to the area by Captain John Mason in his land grant. Before the Revolution, New Hampshire men seized the British fort at Portsmouth in 1774, and in 1775, drove the English governor out. New Hampshire patriots are credited with the first aggressive act of the Revolution, when in 1774, a small group captured Fort William and Mary in New Castle and removed the powder and guns. In 1784, New Hampshire was the first state to adopt its own constitution. New Hampshire was the ninth state of the original thirteen colonies and was the deciding state to ratify the Federal Constitution on June 21, 1788.

State Symbols

New Hampshire's state flower is the purple lilac; its state bird, the purple finch. The state tree is the white birch. New Hampshire's state animal is the white-tailed deer; its insect is the lady bug. Its state song is "Old New Hampshire;" its motto,"Live Free or Die."

New Jersey

The Garden State

Trenton became the state capital of New Jersey in 1790 because of its adjacency to the Delaware River which it overlooks. The first Capitol building was a simpler, two-story structure. It was destroyed by fire in 1885. The present Capitol completed in 1889, is the second oldest state house in continuous use in the United States.

The Capitol building, a solid looking, government office style structure, is an example of the French Academic Classical Revival style of architecture. It is constructed of brick masonry and faced with light-colored Indiana oolitic stone. The foundation and trim are of New Jersey freestone. The building is faced with a double portico supported by granite columns with Corinthian capitals. The state seal embedded in the wall above the balcony on the second portico. A 145 foot high, gold-covered dome crowns the massive building that faces a city street and is the focal point for the historic district surrounding it. A tall, narrow lantern housing with a gold-covered dome is atop the dome. The inside rotunda is the focal point as golden tiers rise and architecturally depict the many layers of history contained within the Capitol.

State History

New Jersey was inhabited by the Lenni Lenape or Delaware Indians prior to the coming of European explorers Giovanni de Verrazano in 1524 and later Henry Hudson in 1609 who claimed the land for the Dutch. By 1623 the land was called New Netherlands and was a busy trading center. In 1664, England gained control, and Charles II gave the area to Lord Berkeley and Sir George Carteret. After years of dispute between Quakers who obtained the western part in 1676 and non-Quakers over the lands in the Jersey, the people were reunited under a government of a royal governor. During this period the population increased dramatically. The divergent views of government and the area's dependence not on England but rather on New York and Philadelphia, drove the populous toward independence.

Independence was declared in June, 1776, and the colony adopted a state constitution. Over 100 battles were fought in New Jersey during the Revolution with the Battles of Trenton, after which Washington retreated across the Hudson to New Jersey, Princeton, and Monmouth the more important ones. Washington's army spent the winters of 1777 and 1778-1779 at Morristown. At the Constitutional Convention, New Jersey delegates prevailed with the Jersey Plan which championed the small states and brought about the Senate in the new government. On December 18, 1787, New Jersey was the third of the original thirteen colonies to ratify the Constitution. During the Civil War the state was on the Union side and provided money and troops.

State Symbols

New Jersey's state bird is the eastern goldfinch; its state flower, the purple violet. The state tree is the red oak. The state animal is the horse; the insect, the honey bee. The state motto is "Liberty and Prosperity." New Jersey was named in honor of Sir George Carteret from the island of Jersey where the Royalists fled after the disposition of Charles I of England.

New Mexico

Land of Enchantment

The New Mexico State Capitol building in Santa Fe is one of the newest as well as one of the most unusual of all state capitols. Its low, round, kiva-like design is patterned after the Zia Pueblo Indian sun symbol, the official emblem of New Mexico, with its four entrances to the building depicting the four rays of the symbol. It was started in 1964 and completed in 1967 at a cost of over $5 million. The old State Capitol is now a state office building in the same complex of state buildings. The simple square columns that go around the building support a high ceiling. The tan adobe-like stucco on the outside imitate the Indian adobe. The rotunda in the center of the building rises to sixty feet and is faced with marble quarried on the Laguna Indian Reservation. The state seal is cast in the terrazzo floor of the rotunda.

Santa Fe has the oldest public building in the U. S., the Palace of Governors built in 1610. It served as headquarters for various governments through the years including the New Mexico Territorial government after 1850.

State History

New Mexico has a centuries old Indian culture and history dating back 12,000 years. In 1536, the first European, Cabeza de Vaca, entered the area. It was explored in 1539 by a Franciscan friar, Marcos de Niza. In 1540, Coronado led explorers searching for El Dorado and the Golden Cities of the Seven Cities of Cibola for Spain. In 1582, a Spanish merchant, Antonio de Espejo, established the Camino Real, the King's Highway from Mexico to Santa Fe. The area remained a Spanish colony until 1821 when Mexico declared its independence and New Mexico area became a province of Mexico. Commerce with the U. S. and the influence of Anglo culture brought about a decline in dependence upon Mexico with the establishing of the Santa Fe Trail to the Missouri area.

During the Mexican War in 1846, Colonel Stephen Kearny's troops occupied Santa Fe and declared the territory a part of the U. S. It was ceded to the U. S. in 1848 and in 1850 became the Territory of New Mexico along with what is now Arizona.

During the Civil War, New Mexico was the Western battleground between Union and Confederate forces. After the war, Indian wars continued and were finally over when U. S. forces defeated Geronimo in 1886. The railroad brought economic growth and the territory's development culminated with New Mexico becoming the 47th. state on January 6, 1912.

State Symbols

New Mexico's state bird is the chaparral or roadrunner; its state flower, the yucca. The state tree is the pinon; the grass, bluegramma grass. New Mexico's animal is the black bear; the fish, the cutthroat trout. Its fossil is the coelophysis; the gem, turquoise. The state vegetable is pinto bean and chili. The state song is "O Fair New Mexico;" the state motto, "It Grows as It Goes."

New York

The Empire State

New York's State Capitol building, completed in 1898 at Albany, is a dignified, massive building done in Renaissance Romanesque Gothic style architecture. It is the second capitol built in Albany. Its construction of Maine granite sets it in stark contrast to the modern buildings surrounding it in Governor Nelson Rockefeller Empire Plaza. The colorful, undulating-appearing surface of the walk in front of the Capitol adds to the contrast.

Approaching the classical five story Gothic structure, its image is reflected in the huge pool before it. The red tile corner roofs and great gray slate roofs with high, ornate dormers give the Capitol building a Medieval European look. The rounded Romanesque arches seen in the window casings on the exterior become the dominant feature of the interior. The outside West staircase rises to the second floor and at one hundred feet wide at the base, is on of the largest in the world. The lobbies of the various entrances are vaults of intersecting arches not unlike those of an ancient monastery. Staircases are an array of the stonecutter's art with animals and intricate designs carved on them.

State History

In 1609, Henry Hudson sailed up the Hudson River to the site of Albany and claimed the area for the Dutch. That same year, Samuel

86

de Champlain discovered Lake Champlain and claimed what is now northern and western New York for the French. By 1624, the Dutch had a permanent settlement at Albany and a fur trading posts extending to Manhattan Island. The Dutch and the English wrestled for control with the English winning out in 1674. New York was named after an English county and town.

In the late 1600's and early 1700's, the Indian Confederacy determined the balance of power between the French and English. England's triumph in the French and Indian War with the capture of Forts Ticonderoga and Niagara and the fall of Montreal brought the war to an end and the loss of power by the Indian Confederation.

Many Revolutionary battles were fought in New York. The British occupied New York after the Battle of Long Island. Following the Battle of White Plains, Washington withdrew to New Jersey. The British tried to take Albany, but met resistance. Later General Burgoyne surrendered at Saratoga. With the surrender of the British at Yorktown in 1781, Washington established his headquarters at Newburg, New York. He took his oath of office as President in 1789 in New York City. New York became the eleventh of the original thirteen states to ratify the Constitution on July 25, 1788.

During the Civil War, New York sent a half-million men to Union forces. The war changed the state into an industrial power.

State Symbols

New York's state bird is the Eastern bluebird; its flower, the rose. The state tree is the sugar maple; the fruit, the apple. Its animal is the American beaver; the fish, the brook or speckled trout. The state fossil is *eurypterus remipes*; the state gem is the garnet. Its motto is "Excelsior, Ever Upward."

The Great Western staircase, built in 1896, is the epitome of stone cutting art. The Million Dollar staircase, medieval in its atmosphere, has stone portraits of famous New Yorkers.

North Carolina

Tar Heel State

The North Carolina State Capitol at Raleigh is one of the best preserved examples of a major civic building in the Greek Revival style of architecture. The Capitol building was completed in 1840 on the site of the original State House that burned in 1831.

Many of the details of the building are patterned after details of ancient Greek temples. The Doric style is seen in the exterior columns of the two deep porticoes that support pediments with entablatures patterned after those of the Parthenon. The rather flat dome is topped by an unusual honeysuckle crown. The House of Representative chambers is patterned after a Greek theater in the the ornamental Corinthian style while the Senate chambers is decorated in the Ionic style of the Erechtheum. The central round rotunda stands 97 1/2 feet high and is at the center of the cross-shaped building. The dome is of copper. The exterior walls are of gneiss, a type of granite that was quarried near Raleigh. The interior walls are stone and brick and the roof is carried by means of a massive, wooden truss system.

State History

North Carolina was one of the earliest areas in the new world to be settled by the English. Sir Walter Raleigh established the first settlement at Fort Raleigh on Roanoke Island in 1585 and 1587. Here in 1587, Virginia Dare became the first English person born in America. The colony vanished and it wasn't until 1664 that colonists from Virginia made a permanent settlement with a grant from Charles II. This grant was withdrawn in 1729 and North Carolina reverted to a crown colony.

The colony's population increased rapidly with the immigration of German and Irish-Scottish settlers. The colony was very active in the Revolution with North Carolina becoming the first colony to authorize their representatives to the Continental Congress to separate from England. On November 21, 1789, North Carolina became the twelfth colony of the original thirteen to ratify the Constitution.

North Carolina seceded and fought on the side of the Confederacy in the Civil War, contributing heavily in manpower and suffering a fourth of the South's casualties. It was restored to the Union in 1868.

State Symbols

North Carolina's state bird is the eastern cardinal or redbird; its flower, the dogwood. The state tree is the pine; the rock, granite. The state's insect is the honeybee; the mammal, the gray squirrel. The official saltwater fish is the channel bass or red drum; the reptile, the turtle. The state shell is the Scotch bonnet; the stone, the emerald. The state's motto is "To Be, Rather Than to Seem." The state song is "The Old North State."

North Dakota

The Sioux State, The Flickertail State

The white, Indiana limestone, nineteen-story 241 foot eight inch high Capitol building in Bismarck, stands in striking contrast against the blue North Dakota skies on a base of Wisconsin black granite. The Capitol was constructed in the early 1930's at only $2 million and is one of the nation's most practical and economically built capitols.

The interior is a blend of foreign and domestic stone and wood. Memorial Hall combines black Belgium marble with Montana yellowstone travertine walls along with Tennessee marble floors. The room features forty foot bronze pillars and window frames. Rooms are paneled with exotic woods such as Honduras mahogany, East Indian rosewood and laurel wood, English brown oak, maple, American chestnut, and Burma teak. Many of these materials are used in the Art Deco styling of the interior of the building. Art Deco characteristics are found in the stylized light fixtures; dentil frieze, a band of tooth-like ribbing, located where walls meet the ceiling; and repeated vertical lines or ribbing on pillars, walls, ceiling, doors, and windows. Another characteristic is the base relief or raised sculpture found on revolving doors.

State History

The area that is North Dakota was almost unexplored until 1738 when a Canadian fur trader, Pierre La Verendrye, explored the area. Half the area was part of the Louisiana Purchase in 1803, and Lewis and Clark explored it and built Fort Mandan. The first permanent settlement was made near Pembina in 1812 by Canadians under Lord Selkirk. In 1818, the other half of the area was transferred to the U. S. by the British

The Indian Wars that sweep the plains for three decades prevented settlement. The most famous battle occurred in 1876 when General George Custer led the 7th. Cavalry to the Little Big Horn where the Sioux wiped out his entire company. Finally, in 1881, Sitting Bull surrendered, peace came, and homesteading accelerated, aided by the building of the railroads in the territories.

The Dakota Territory was organized in 1861. It included both North and South Dakota areas. A political battle for the capital began, and finally, in 1883, Bismarck was selected. The situation was resolved when the two halves of the Territory were admitted to the Union on November 2, 1889, as North and South Dakota, the 39th. and 40 th. states.

State Symbols

North Dakota's state flower is the wild prairie rose; its bird, the Western meadowlark. The state tree is the American elm; its grass, the Western wheat grass. The state beverage is milk; the state fossil is teredo petrified wood. The state song is "North Dakota Hymn." North Dakota's motto is "Liberty and union, now and forever, one and inseparable." The name Dakota comes from the Dakota or Sioux Indians and means "allies."

Ohio

The Buckeye State

The long, low white limestone Ohio State House in downtown Columbus is one of the finest examples of Greek Doric architecture in the United States. The cornerstone was laid in 1839 and the building was completed in 1861 after fourteen years of political feuding about the location of a state capital. The city of Columbus was begun by the residents of Franklinton, a town across the river from where the Capitol was constructed. It was designated the state capital in 1816. Eventually, Columbus became the economic center and literally surrounded the original city of Fanklinton. Today the Capitol building is surrounded by skyscrapers in the center of Columbus.

The center rotunda dominates the building which is noted for its fine thirty-six foot high, six foot thick Doric columns at each of the four entrances. The limestone for the marble interior was quarried near Columbus. The flat-roofed, round cupola has modified Doric pilasters around it and rises 158 feet above ground level. A modified pediment breaks up the roundness of the structure. Inside the floor of the rotunda is inlaid marble and a lighted painting of the Ohio seal hangs in the dome 120 feet above.

State History

The state of Ohio area was settled as far back in history as 800 B. C. by Indians known as the Moundbuilders. It was the Frenchman, LaSalle, who visited the area in 1669. American fur traders arrived in 1685. The territory was a constant battleground between England and France. The French were driven out in 1763 and ceded the area to the British after the French and Indian War.

During the Revolution, Indian frontier wars went on with the area becoming a U. S. territory after the Revolution. The conflict with the Indians continued until 1794, when General Anthony Wayne defeated the Indian Confederation at Fallen Timbers, ending Indian warfare with a treaty signed at Greenville in 1795. After the Northwest Territory was created in 1787, the first organized settlement was established at Marietta in Ohio in 1788. During the War of 1812, Oliver Perry defeated the British on Lake Erie and William Harrison invaded Canada. Ohio entered the Union on March 1, 1803, as the 17th. state and was the first state formed from the Northwest Territory.

State Symbols

The Ohio state flower is the red carnation; its state bird, the cardinal. The state animal is the white-tailed deer; the state insect, the ladybug renamed the Ladybird Beetle. The state tree is the buckeye; the gem, Ohio flint. The Ohio fossil is the isotelus or trilobite. Ohio's official beverage is tomato juice. The state song is "Beautiful Ohio;" its motto is "With God, all things are possible." The state Rock song is "Hang on, Sloopy." The name Ohio comes from the Iroquois word "O-he-yo" meaning "great river.

Oklahoma

The Sooner State

The Oklahoma State Capitol building at Oklahoma City has the symbol of the state, an oil derrick, set in a petunia flower bed near the front steps. The well, Petunia One, was started in November, 1941, making Oklahoma's Classic Greco-Roman capitol the only state capitol building with an oil well under it. At one time it produced 600 barrels of oil a day. The long four story white Indiana limestone building is fronted by Roman Corinthian columns set in a colonnade across the entire structure. These support a classic portico with a pediment with a plain entablature. On each roof corner of the portico are stylized, winged lions. The east and west facades have Corinthian pilasters. The base of the building is of Oklahoma pink and black granite. The floors are of Alabama marble and the stairs and wall bases are of Vermont marble. The state seal set in the floor of the rotunda is 105 feet below a matching seal that is surrounded by leaded glass art work set in the ceiling.

State History

Spanish explorers, Coronado in 1541 and del Castillo, were early visitors to the Oklahoma area. In 1719, Bernard de la Harpe, a French explorer, came to eastern Oklahoma. Oklahoma was part of the Louisiana Purchase in 1803 and many expeditions followed.

The modern history of the Oklahoma area began in 1830 when Congress declared that all Indians east of the Mississippi River be relocated in what was declared as Indian Territory, the home of the Five Tribes: Cherokee, Choctaw, Chickasaw, Creek, and Seminole between 1828-1846. They established a constitution and a formal type of government. The Civil War found their internal conflicts becoming worse, as they fought on both sides of the conflict, with most favoring the Confederate side. After the war, governmental regulations for reservations and the coming of the railroad hemmed in the Indians further. In 1890, the area became the Oklahoma Territory.

Finally, with the premature coming of the "Sooners," who were settlers that sneaked across boundaries prior to land being opened up for settlement, and then the runs to newly homesteaded lands in the Territory, the first one taking place in 1889, brought an end to Indian domination of the area. The most famous run was to the Cherokee Outlet in 1893. By 1904, all surplus Indian land had been distributed and the Indian Territory in the east and the western Oklahoma Territory united to form Oklahoma as the 46th. state on November 6, 1907.

State Symbols

Oklahoma's state flower is the mistletoe; the wildflower, the Indian blanket. Its state bird, the scissor-tailed flycatcher; the animal, the American bison. The state tree is the redbud; the state grass, Indian grass. The state fish is the white bass; the state reptile, the collared lizard. Oklahoma's state song is "Oklahoma;" the state instrument, the fiddle. The state rock is Barite rose. Oklahoma's state motto is "Labor conquers all things." The state poem, "Howdy, Folks" by David Milstern. The name for Oklahoma derives from two Choctaw words, "okla" meaning "people" and "humma" meaning "red."

Oregon

The Beaver State

Oregon's State Capitol building in Salem is one of utmost simplicity in line and form. It is the third capitol building on the site. The first Capitol, erected in 1854, was destroyed by fire as was the second Capitol, patterned after the U. S. capitol, and completed in 1876. It burned in 1935.

The present Capitol was dedicated in 1938 and is the only WPA Capitol project in the U. S. The four-story structure of modern Greek architecture has a starkness that belies its simplicity. The shell is a combination of reinforced steel and concrete with the exterior faced with white marble from the Danby quarry in Vermont. The interior is faced with rose travertine from Montana, and the floor and staircases of the rotunda are Phoenix Napoleon grey marble from Missouri with borders of black marble from Vermont. The exterior simplicity is carried out in the interior that has little decoration. The staircases are square instead of the usual curved arch. All exterior doors and windows are made of bronze. The central dome rises 106 feet and has a flat-topped lantern ringed by modified 'antae.' It is topped by the twenty-four foot, bronze, gold-covered sculpture the "Oregon Pioneer," an heroic figure representing the spirit of Oregon's early settlers. The statue's base is 140 feet above ground level.

State History

Oregon was first seen by white men when in 1543, Bartolome Ferrelo, a Spanish explorer sailed up the coast. In 1774, another Spanish explorer, Juan Perez, sailed along the coast. He was followed by Captain Cook who also sailed along the coast in 1778. In 1792, an American, Robert Gray, discovered the Colombia River. Then in 1805, Lewis and Clark arrived and spent the winter on the coast. Fur traders followed Lewis and Clark and by 1834, settlers started arriving with the first real influx coming in 1843 via the Oregon Trail.

After years of dispute over the area, the U. S. and Britain signed a treaty in 1846, setting the 49º N. latitude as the International boundary. In 1849, the portion south of the Columbia River became the Territory of Oregon with a capitol at Oregon City. Oregon became the 33rd. state, entering the Union on February 14, 1859.

State Symbols

Oregon's state flower is the Oregon grape; its bird, the Western meadowlark. The state tree is the Douglas fir; the animal, the beaver. The Oregon state fish is the Chinook salmon; the insect, the swallowtail butterfly. The state rock is thunderegg. The state song, "Oregon, My Oregon." Oregon's motto is a single statement "The Union." The name "Oregon" was first used by Major Robert Rogers in 1765 in a petition to the British government.

Pennsylvania

The Keystone State

The Pennsylvania State Capitol building completed in 1906 in Harrisburg is a striking adaptation of Italian Renaissance architecture. The dome, supported by paired Corinthian columns and patterned after the Cathedral of St. Peter's in Rome, rises 272 feet and is topped by a female statue representing the Commonwealth, and nicknamed "Miss Penn." The 52 million pound dome is supported by four pillars sunk seven feet in a natural bed of slate rock. The pillars are over twenty-nine feet in diameter at their base and taper to over twelve feet at the point of support. The columned porticoes in front are Corinthian order. The five-story building has a tiled, green-glazed roof and an exterior of Vermont granite.

The monumental rotunda features an Italian marble staircase that curves upward left and right and is patterned after the grand stairway in the Opera House in Paris. It is balanced visually with two statues holding lights at the base and four Corinthian pilasters at the stairs ascent. Curved balustrade balconies on either side add to the total balance. The interior rooms have the three architectural orders displayed in the ornamental wall pilasters. The Corinthian order is used in the House of Representatives, the dignified Doric is displayed in the Senate, and the Ionic order is used in the Supreme Court chambers. The ornate Corinthian is also displayed in the grand tier upward through the dome. It is the paintings of Edwin Austin Abbey in the House that are of special note. His "Apotheosis," "Penn's Treaty with the Indians," and "Reading of the Declaration of Independence" are highly valued.

State History

Pennsylvania was first claimed by the Dutch because of Henry Hudson's 1609 expedition. Swedish colonies followed in 1637, and the first permanent settlement was made on Tinicum Island. In 1655, the Dutch seized the settlement but lost it to the British in 1664. In 1681, Charles II gave a charter to the Quaker William Penn who established a colony for religious freedom.

Prior to the Revolution there was a great influx of settlers from Germany, the Pennsylvania Dutch, and from Britain. Philadelphia was not only the colony's center of government, but it was the capital of the colonies during most of the Revolution. The First and Second Continental Congress met in Philadelphia where the The Declaration of Independence, 1776, and the Constitution, 1787, were signed. Philadelphia served as the nation's capital from 1790 to 1800. Pennsylvania was the second of the original thirteen colonies to ratify the Constitution on December 12, 1787.

During the Civil War, the Battle of Gettysburg was fought in the state and the tide turned for the Union. Here Lincoln stated the purposes of the Union in his "Gettysburg Address."

State Symbols

Pennsylvania's state flower is the mountain laurel; its state bird, the ruffed grouse. The state animal is the whitetailed deer; the state fish, the brook trout. The Great Dane is the state dog; the firefly, the state insect.. The state tree is the hemlock. Pennsylvania's state motto is "Virtue, liberty, and independence." Charles II named Pennsylvania in honor of William Penn's father. It means "Penn's woods."

Rhode Island

The Ocean State; Little Rhody

The gleaming white Georgia marble State House of Rhode Island overlooks the city of Providence from the crest of Smith Hill. It is Rhode Island's seventh capitol. Until 1854, legislative sessions were held throughout the state. The three story, 235 foot, domed Capitol was begun in 1895 and completed and occupied in 1904. The Capitol's design is based on St. Paul's Cathedral in London, the U. S. Capitol, and City Hall in New York City. It is 235 feet high from the terrace to the top of the statue that sets on the second largest, self-supporting marble dome in the world.

The sculpture by George Brewster is an allegorical representation of the "Independent Man." On either side of the dome are saucer domes over each of the legislative chambers. Four smaller domes supported by Corinthian colonnades are at the corners below the main dome.

The interior rooms of the Capitol are in the tradition of marbled halls and marble-columned, ornamental rooms in European buildings. Hanging in the State Room is Gilbert Stuart's portrait of George Washington. The three architectural orders are shown throughout the Capitol. The exterior columns are Corinthian; the ornate State Room and Senate chamber have Ionic decorative pilasters; while the House of Representatives is surrounded by large Doric columns.

State History

The first European to visit the area of Rhode Island was a Dutchman, Adrian Block, in 1614. Rhode Island was founded by many who sought individual liberty. The first were dissidents from Massachusetts Bay Colony led by Roger Williams in 1636. Two years later in 1638, Anne Hutchinson, her husband, and a group led by William Coddington and John Clarke left Massachusetts and founded Portsmouth. In 1642, Samuel Gorton fled Massachusetts and founded Warwick. In 1663, Roger Williams led the towns to seek a charter from Charles II. It was granted that year as the Colony of Rhode Island and the Providence Plantations. This charter was the basis of government until 1842.

Rhode Island's peace with the Indians was maintained while New England Indian wars were being fought. In 1675-76, King Philip's War occurred and ended with King Philip's death. In 1776, Rhode Island was the first colony to renounce allegiance to England. Prior to this declaration, they had burned two British ships near Warwick. This occurred before the Concord and Lexington battles starting the Revolution. Newport was blockaded for three years during the war. Rhode Island was the thirteenth state to ratify the Constitution on May 19, 1790. Industrialization came after the war. The first power loom in the U. S. was started in 1814. During the Civil War, support for the Union and anti-slavery sentiments were strong within the state.

State Symbols

Rhode Island's state flower is the violet; the state bird, the Rhode Island red chicken. The state tree is the red maple; the mineral, bowenite; the state rock is cumberlandite. The state song is "Rhode Island;" its motto is the single word "Hope."

South Carolina

The Palmetto State

South Carolina's classical Capitol in Columbia is constructed in the Italian Renaissance style. Construction began in 1786 with the cornerstone laid in 1851. Most of the granite for the Capitol was quarried from the Granby quarry two miles south of the building. The domeless Capitol of the 19th. century was partially burned by General Sherman in 1865 and today the ten cannon balls that struck the building are marked by brass markers. In 1885-1891, rebuilding was started again using original plans. Then in 1900, the roof was replaced and the three tiered dome, lantern housing, and porticoes were added. The plain pediment is supported by Corinthian columns.

In the House of Representatives, a solid silver mace made in London in 1756 is on display and used only for ceremonial events. The room is paneled with Vermont Verde marble.

State History

Of the original thirteen colonies, South Carolina was one of the first to be colonized, it was a battleground in the Revolutionary War, and it was the first state to secede from the Union prior to the Civil War. It was the Spanish who attempted the first settlement in 1526 near Georgetown. In 1562, the Huguenots attempted a settlement near Beaufort which was later abandoned. Then in 1670, English nobles, given charters by Charles II, established provinces in the areas of North and South Carolina.

In spite of a strong Loyalist group in the state, South Carolinians were leaders in the Revolution. Two important battles were King's Mountain in 1780, and at the Cowpens, 1781. Before the war's end, 137 battles and skirmishes were fought on South Carolina soil. On May 23, 1788, South Carolina became the eighth state to ratify the Constitution.

In 1860, the Ordinance of Secession made South Carolina the first state to secede. The Battle of Fort Sumter in Charleston harbor marked the start of the Civil War when it was captured by the Confederates. Few battles were fought in the state, but General Sherman on his march to the sea passed through South Carolina, burning and destroying everything in his way. The coastal towns fell to the Union forces with Charleston being the target of a blockade and shelling.

State Symbols

South Carolina's state flower is the yellow jasmine; its bird, the Carolina wren. The state tree is the palmetto and the state animal is the white-tailed deer. The state's gem stone is the amethyst; the stone, blue granite. South Carolina's state fish is the striped bass; the wild game bird is the wild turkey. The state fruit is the peach, and the state drink, milk. The state dog is the Boykin spaniel, a hunting dog originally bred by South Carolinians. The state mottoes are "While I breathe, I hope;" and "Prepared in Mind and Resources." Carolina is derived from Carolus, the Latin word of Charles, honoring Charles II.

South Dakota

The Sunshine State

Pierre was chosen as the state capital of South Dakota in 1904 and the South Dakota legislature proceeded to fund monies for the Capitol building which was built from 1907-10. It is a Neoclassical Roman Renaissance design with the exterior of Marquette raindrop sandstone and Indiana Bedford limestone with the foundation of South Dakota boulder granite. The Capitol dome, done in Italian Renaissance style, is copper, rising 161 feet above the ground. The four small decorative porticoes divide the Corinthian colonnade in the drum of the dome. A lantern housing with a ball on top rises above a round porch at its base. Interesting features of the structure are the series of balustrades around the roof line and plain pediments at the corners and the ends. The front modified portico is supported by Corinthian columns.

The elaborate interior features Greek and Roman designs, murals, and stenciling done in ivory, blue, tan, and gold hues to harmonize with the marble wainscotting, columns, and terrazzo tile floor. The rotunda is ninety-six feet high and features colored Victorian glass.

State History

South Dakota has a long history of Indian culture dating back to the Moundbuilders who inhabited the land as far back in history as 800 A.D. The Verendrye brothers were the first known European explorers to visit the state in 1742-43. Then in 1804 and 1806, Lewis and Clark moved through the area on their exploration of the Louisiana Purchase. The fur trade led to the establishment of a series of trading posts along the Missouri River. Fort Pierre, opposite Pierre, was one of the trading posts.

The first American settlement was at Sioux Falls in 1859, but the Indian wars prevented a permanent settlement. Congress established the Dakota Territory in 1861. It was the railroad that made the territory accessible to settlers. Then in 1874, gold was discovered on the Sioux Reservation and a mining rush was on. At first, the U.S. attempted to stop the influx which was a violation of a treaty with the Indians, but then it relaxed its opposition when gold in great quantities was confirmed. Indian warfare broke out and reached a peak when General Custer was defeated by the Sioux at Little Big Horn in 1876. A year later the Sioux gave up the land.

The influx of prospectors and European farmers swelled the population. Political turmoil broke out between the northern and southern settlers over the location of the capital of the territory. Resolution came when the territory was divided and two Dakotas were admitted to the Union on November 2, 1889, with South Dakota the 40th. state to enter the Union. The final Indian uprising, the Messiah War in 1890, ended with the massacre of Indian families at Wounded Knee.

State Symbols

South Dakota's state flower is the pasque flower; its state bird, the ringnecked pheasant. The state tree is the Black Hills spruce. The coyote is the state animal; the fish, the walleye. The state insect is the honeybee; the grass is Western wheat grass. The official state gem is Fairburn agate; the mineral is rose agate. South Dakota's state motto is "Under God, the people rule." "Hail, South Dakota" is the state song. The state is named after the Dakota Indians.

Tennessee

The Volunteer State

Tennessee's State Capitol stands on a commanding site in the city of Nashville. The 206 feet high Capitol building is modeled after a Greek Ionic temple. The cornerstone was laid in 1845, and the building completed in 1859. The four Ionic porticoes resemble the Erectheum in Athens. A colonnade of eight Ionic columns on each end support a plain pediment. The two-tiered tower with Corinthian pilasters supporting a crown ring is patterned after the Choragic Monument of Lysicrates in Athens. The structure was originally constructed of stone from a nearby quarry, but in the 1950's, restoration was done using Indiana limestone for the steps, terraces, columns, and other parts of the building.

The original inside terra cotta colors and ceiling paintings have been restored. The House of Representatives has a ceiling supported by sixteen fluted Ionic columns. The tomb of President James A. Polk is on the grounds.

State History

The Cherokee Indians were the first civilized inhabitants of Tennessee. Exploration of the area occurred when Hernando De Soto, the Spanish explorer who discovered the Mississippi River in 1541, stopped near today's Memphis. The Spanish did not claim the area and so later it became an area of contention between the French and the British during the French and Indian War. Prior to the Revolution, many settlers moved into the area from the Virginia and Carolina areas.

The first permanent settlement west of the Alleghenies was in 1768 in the northeast part of the state. In 1772, the Watauga Association was established by settlers from the Virginias. In 1776, Tennessee settlers went on the side of the American patriots and became a part of North Carolina area. North Carolina ceded its western lands to the U. S. in 1784, but the Watauga settlers rebelled and formed the state of Franklin. It existed for 4 years. In 1789, North Carolina ceded the territory south of the Ohio River to Congress. Later, Tennessee became the 16th. state on June 1, 1796.

In 1843, Nashville was designated the permanent capital. Tennessee was the last state to secede from the Union in 1861, but it still sent troops to the Confederate and Union armies. During the war, 454 battles and skirmishes were fought in Tennessee with Shiloh, Stones River, Chickamauga, and Chattanooga, major battles. Tennessee was the first state to reenter the Union on July 24, 1866.

State Symbols

Tennessee's state flower is the iris; its state bird, the mockingbird. The state tree is the tulip poplar. The official state rock is limestone; the gem, the Tennessee pearl. The state insects are the firefly and the lady bug; the wild animal, the raccoon. The state song is"The Tennessee Waltz;" the folk dance, the square dance. The official art is porcelain painting. The state's motto is,"Agriculture and Commerce." "Tennessee" is perhaps derived from the Cherokee Indians' ancient capital named Tannansie or Tansi.

Texas

The Lone Star State

The impressive Texas Capitol located in Austin is a Classical copper-roofed structure built between 1882-1888 in the shape of a Grecian cross. When completed, it was the seventh largest building in the world. The dome, patterned after the nation's Capitol, is 309 feet, 8 inches high, seven feet higher than the National Capitol. There are two levels of balconies. At a lower level is a balustrade supporting Corinthian columns that in turn support an circular balustrade and open balcony. Atop the lantern housing is the sixteen foot high statue, Goddess of Liberty, holding the Lone Star in her raised hand.

The Capitol's exterior walls are Texas pink granite quarried at Marble Falls. The interior and dome walls are Texas limestone. The rotunda rises four floors to a sky-blue ceiling with the Texas Lone Star in the center. The Capitol's south foyer floor memorializes the twelve major battles fought on Texas soil. In the center of the rotunda floor is a terrazzo design of the "Seal of Nations," showing the five nations that have ruled Texas. Around the Seal of the Republic of Texas are the Great Seal of the United States, the Seal of the Confederacy, the Seal of Mexico, the fleur-de-lis of the French coat of arms, and the Seal of Spain.

State History

The Spanish were the first to explore Texas. Cabeza de Vaca was one of the first in 1528. In the 1550's, Coronado and de Soto arrived in search of gold. By 1682, Spain attempted a permanent settlement at Ysleta, near El Paso. The Frenchman, de La Salle, led an expedition in 1685. To prevent the French from settling, Spain established missions in the south-central area. From these grew the towns of Goliad, Nacogdoches, and San Antonio. At the start of the 19th. century these were the only settlements of note in Texas with San Antonio the largest.

By 1821, Mexico, which included Texas, broke free from Spain. It offered generous land grants to settle the territory. Stephen Austin led 300 American families into Texas and within 15 years Americans outnumbered the Mexicans. In 1832, Austin carried a petition for self-government to Santa Anna, but was jailed and then released. Austin returned, starting the Texas Revolution in 1835. After several victories, the Americans were defeated at the Alamo in San Antonio and at Goliad. With "Remember the Alamo" as a battle cry, the Americans, led by Sam Houston, defeated Santa Anna at San Jacinto in 1836.

From 1836 to 1845, the Republic of Texas was an independent nation. Later December 29, 1845, Texas joined the Union as the 28th. state. This started the Mexican War, 1846-1848, in which General Zachary Taylor moved forces into disputed Western territory as far as the Rio Grande River. Later after U. S. forces drove victoriously into Mexico, the war

ended with the Treaty of Guadelupe-Hidalgo signed on February 2, 1848. During the Civil War, Texas was the second state to secede from the Union in 1861; it rejoined in 1870.

State Symbols

The Texas state flower is the bluebonnet; the state bird, the mockingbird. The state tree is the pecan; the state song, "Texas, Our Texas." A Lone Star is the most important symbol. The Texas motto is the word, "Friendship." The name Texas is derived from "Tejas," a Spanish name for the Hasinai Indians.

Utah

The Beehive State

Utah's State Capitol is situated on Salt Lake City's northern foothills of the Wasatch Mountains overlooking the city and valley. The structure was completed in 1915, fifteen years after Utah became a state. The Capitol building is patterned after the U. S. Capitol in Washington and is one of the finest examples of Classical Renaissance Revival architecture in the United States.

The imposing building is faced with an unadorned pediment over a portico supported by seven Corinthian columns which continue in a colonnade across the front of the rest of the building. It is constructed of Utah granite on the exterior and of white Georgia marble on the interior. The Renaissance style copper-covered dome rises over 285 feet and is supported by Corinthian columns holding the drum of the dome. An open circular balcony encircles the dome. The interior rotunda rises 165 feet from the floor to a ceiling decorated with sea gulls, Utah's state bird. Each bird has a six foot wing span. Suspended from the center of the rotunda ceiling is a 3,200 pound brass chandelier, hanging by a 95 foot chain. The state reception room or "Gold Room" is noted for its 23-karat Utah gold leaf adornment. Golden Traverse marble around the fireplaces and walkway is most unusual with its sixteen distinctive colors including gold.

State History

Captain Cardenas, a Spanish explorer with Coronado, was the first European to visit the area in 1540. Later in 1776, Spanish missionaries entered Utah trying to find a land route from Santa Fe to Monterey, California, another Franciscan mission. They are credited with discovering the Green River. For many years Utah was the scene for fur trappers. Trappers led by William Ashley traveled throughout the area, and in 1824, two trappers, James Bridger and Etieene Provost, discovered the Great Salt Lake.

In 1847, the Great Salt Lake Valley, which was still Mexican territory, was settled by 143 Mormons from Illinois led by Brigham Young in July, 1847. Other Mormons followed and by the end of 1847, more than 2,000 had settled in the Valley. The United States gained the territory in 1848 through the Treaty of Guadalupe Hidalgo which ended the Mexican War. The Mormon settlers then set up a provisional government called the state of Deseret with Young as governor. In 1850, the United States created the Territory of Utah. After the outlawing of polygamy in its constitution, Utah attained statehood on January 4, 1896 as the 45th. state.

State Symbols

The Utah state flower is the sego lily; its bird, the seagull. The state tree is the blue spruce. The state animal is the elk; the fish is the rainbow trout. The state gem is topaz. Utah's insect is the honeybee with the beehive the official state emblem. Utah's single word motto is "Industry." The state song is "Utah, We Love Thee." Utah is named after the Ute Indian tribe.

Vermont

The Green Mountain State

The present State House of Vermont is the third one located in Montpelier, which became the capital in 1805, on the condition that the town give land for a capitol building that the would be completed by 1808. The first capitol building, built in 1808, deteriorated and was torn down in 1836. The second state house, made of Barre granite from a quarry ten miles away, burned in 1857. The granite columns from the second state house were incorporated into the present building, completed in 1859. The Classical Grecian styled building has a portico of six simple Doric columns designed after the ancient Greek temple of Theseus. The unadorned Doric is in contrast to the more elaborate Ionic and Corinthian columns inside the building. The Capitol's walls are of Vermont granite with Italianate detailed windows. The wooden, copper sheathed, gold-covered dome is fifty-seven feet high. On top of the dome is a statue of Ceres, the Roman goddess of agriculture. Many fossils can be seen in the Isle LaMotte black marble that covers the main lobby floor.

State History

Samuel de Champlain explored the Vermont region in 1609. It remained French until into the mid-1700's when the French abandoned the territory. The first permanent English settlement was in 1724, near the present town of Brattleboro. After the French and Indian War, confusion over which state had a claim to the area occurred. New Hampshire, New York, and Connecticut claimed the area. In 1770, New York tried to get settlers to repurchase their land. Local militia led by Ethan Allen and Remember Baker led the Green Mountain Boys, protecting the settlers and leading the fight against England. They captured Fort Ticonderoga for the colonials. In 1777, they were defeated at Hubbardton, the only Revolutionary battle fought in Vermont. In 1777, a convention at Westminster declared statehood with the name New Connecticut, which was latter changed to Vermont. New York, which prevented statehood for Vermont for 14 years, withdrew its claims in 1789. On March 4, 1791, Vermont became the 14th. state, the first to be admitted under the Constitution.

During the War of 1812, Vermont took an active part, contributing to the British naval defeat on Lake Champlain. Again during the Civil War, Vermont contributed heavily with men and money to the Union cause.

State Symbols

Vermont's state flower is the red clover; its state bird, the hermit thrush. The state tree is the sugar maple; the state animal, the Morgan horse. The state insect is the honeybee; the state vegetable, sweet corn. Vermont's two state fish are the warm water fish, walleye pike; the cold water fish, the brook trout. The state beverage is milk. Vermont's state motto is "Freedom and Unity;" its song, "Hail, Vermont."

Virginia

The Old Dominion State

Thomas Jefferson designed the Virginia Capitol at Richmond, basing it upon the La Maison Caree, a Roman temple in Nimes, France. Its Classical Revival design with huge plain columns with Ionic capitals fronting the building, was the first such structure built in America. In use since 1788, it is today the meeting place of the oldest law-making body in the Western Hemisphere and the first to function under a written constitution of a free people. The Capitol's cornerstone was laid in 1785, but it wasn't completed until 1800 when the outside walls of handmade brick were stuccoed. It served as the capitol of the Confederacy between 1861-1865. Side wings were added in 1904-06.

The checkerboard black and white squares in the rotunda and hall floors are of limestone. The black limestone squares contain sea fossils of snails, sea lilies, algae, corals and nautiloids. In the rotunda is the prized piece of marble sculpture, a life-size statue of George Washington carved from life by Jean Antoine Houdon. Another carved from life bust of Marquis de Lafayette by Houdon is on display along with busts of seven Virginia born presidents, Thomas Jefferson, James Madison, James Monroe, William Harrison, John Tyler, Zachary Taylor, and Woodrow Wilson. The rotunda is covered by an interior dome with a skylight that illuminates the Washington statue. It is ornamented with Renaissance style decorations.

State History

John Cabot was one of the first explorers to visit the area of Virginia in 1497 and establish the basis for English possession. Sir Walter Raleigh established Jamestown in 1607. This colony's government became the basis of the future federal constitutional government of the United States. It was because of English appointed royal governors and the French and Indian War that led Virginians under George Roger Clark to free the Ohio-Indiana-Illinois area from the British. These events led Virginians toward home rule and revolution.

Men such as Patrick Henry, Thomas Jefferson, George Washington, Richard Bland, and Richard Henry Lee encouraged the inhabitants toward independence from the English crown through their writings, speeches, and actions. In 1776, the royal governor were replaced and the assembly adopted the Virginia Declaration of Rights which influenced the United States Constitution. It was in Virginia that Benedict Arnold burned Richmond and Petersburg for the British in 1781, bringing about an American defeat. Later it was at Yorktown in Virginia that Cornwallis was trapped and surrendered.

Virginia was the tenth of the original thirteen colonies to ratify the Constitution on June 25, 1788. During the War of 1812, Virginia harbors and coastline were blockaded by the British.

Virginia was the Civil War battleground in the East. Manassas, The Wilderness, Chancellorsville, and Seven Days were major battles fought on Virginia soil.

State Symbols

Virginia's state flower is the dogwood; its state bird, the cardinal. The state tree is the dogwood; the state song "Carry Me Back to Old Virginia." The state beverage is milk; the dog is the American foxhound. The oyster shell is the official shell. The state motto is "Thus always to tyrants." Sir Walter Raleigh named the state in honor of Elizabeth I, the Virgin Queen.

Jean Antoine Houdon's life-sized statue of George Washington in a classic pose, is one of our Nation's most prized sculptures.

Washington

The Evergreen State

Washington's State Legislative building at Olympia is an example of Corinthian Gothic architecture with a touch of Rococo. The present structure, begun in 1893, is the second official capitol building and is the tallest domed masonry state capitol building in the United States and the fifth tallest in the world. Disputes about size, plans, and location, prevented its completion until 1928.

The exterior of the Capitol is buff-colored Wilkeson sandstone from a quarry forty miles east of Olympia. The rest of the building is constructed of Washington granite from Index. The simple Tuscan columns encircle the building with a colonnade of Corinthian columns supporting the entrance portico displaying a plain pediment. The impressive dome is 287 feet high and at the time of completion was the fourth largest dome in the world. It is circled by Corinthian columns supporting the drum of the dome. The dome is topped by an elaborate, columned-encircled lantern housing. Entrance to the Capitol is through any of six solid bronze doors weighing five tons each. A cast bronze chandelier titled "Angels of Mercy" weighing five tons hangs in the rotunda. All light fixtures, Louis Comfert Tiffany's last major commission, were made by Tiffany Art Studios in 1923.

State History

The search for the fabled Northwest Passage resulted in the discovery of the area that is now Washington. The Washington coast was explored by the Spanish in 1775, followed later by British explorers. In 1792, Englishman George Vancouver explored Puget Sound and an American, Robert Gray, discovered the Columbia River thereby setting up contention for the area. With the Louisiana Purchase, American claims were enhanced and the area was explored by Lewis and Clark in 1805.

The War of 1812 brought about joint occupancy of the area which included Oregon. Settlement of the entire area by American settlers continued until 1843 when supremacy by Americans brought about a British-American Boundary Treaty in 1846, setting the 49th. parallel as the dividing line between the U. S. and Canada. In 1848, the Oregon Territory was established, followed by the Washington Territory in 1853, with Olympia the territorial capital. The 1855 gold rush and the completion of the Northern Pacific Railroad in 1883, were compelling reasons for statehood. Washington became the 42nd. state on November 11, 1889.

State Symbols

Washington's state flower is the Western rhododendron; its state bird, the willow goldfinch. The state tree is the Western hemlock. The official dance is the square dance. The steelhead trout is the official fish; petrified wood, the official gem. "Washington, My Home" is the state song; the state motto is "By and by." The state is named after George Washington.

West Virginia

The Mountain State

The West Virginia gold-domed Capitol at Charleston is the sixth building to serve as the center of government. The classical Renaissance dome supported by a circular colonnade of Corinthian columns rises 293 feet above the Great Kanawha River flowing in front of it. Constructed of limestone and marble, the Capitol building was completed and dedicated in 1932. Limestone Corinthian styled pillars weighing eighty-six tons stand at the north and south entrances. The Corinthian columns support porticoes under which are 2,800 pound brass and copper sliding doors decorated with elm, hickory, beech, and maple leaves representing West Virginian's native hardwood trees. Tuscan styled pilasters are on the building's sides and ends.

In the rotunda beneath the dome hangs a four ton chandelier 180 feet above and made of over 10,000 pieces of Czechoslovakian crystal. Columns of black Belgian marble line the hall on the main level. Interior marbles include Imperial Danby, Italian Travertine, Tennessee, white Vermont, black Belgian, and pink Georgian.

State History

Early Moundbuilders left their marks with effigy mounds built in the region. The area that became the state of West Virginia was on the cutting edge of the wilderness during the 18th. and early 19th. centuries. Morgan Morgan is credited with being the first permanent settler; he arrived in 1726. The areas along the Potomac River and the Shenandoah Valley were explored as early as 1730's by fur traders with the Pennsylvania Germans moving across the Potomac into the area in the years following.

Although the Indian wars held back settlement for a time, by 1775, 30,000 settlers populated the area. While the interior inhabitants participated in the Revolution by battling the Indians, they began to differ from the Virginians on the coast. They owned few slaves and grew more independent. They contributed to the Mexican War and fought in the War of 1812. It was the act of Virginia's secession from the Union in 1861, that brought about the final division when the western part of Virginia secured status as a new state. West Virginia joined the Union in the midst of the Civil War on June 20, 1863, as the 35th. state.

State Symbols

West Virginia's state flower is the big rhododendron; its state bird, the cardinal. The state tree is the sugar maple; the fruit, the apple. The black bear is the state animal; the brook trout the state fish. The state songs are "The West Virginia Hills;" "This is My West Virginia;" and "West Virginia, My Home, Sweet Home." "Mountaineers are always free" is the state motto.

118

Wisconsin

The Badger State

The magnificent Greco-Roman Renaissance cruciform Wisconsin Capitol in downtown Madison, is the second building to occupy the site. Built 1906-1909, its 270 1/4 foot dome, is probably the only granite-covered dome in the United States, and the largest dome by volume ever built in the U. S. and the third largest dome by volume in the world. The building's exterior is built of White Bethel Vermont granite. Each wing is terminated by stately, formal porticoes composed of Corinthian columns supporting pediments whose tympanums display granite statuary. The barrel of the dome is supported by Corinthian columns in a circle arcade. The dome is surrounded by an open granite balustrade. A colonnade of Corinthian columns support the lantern, on which is the 15 1/2 foot gilded bronze Daniel Chester French statue of "Wisconsin," symbolizing the state's motto, "Forward." The state animal, the badger, is on her helmet's crest.

The interior materials of the Capitol are granite, limestone, and marbles from the U. S. and the world. The rotunda rises two hundred feet from the ground floor with the crown of the coffer dome holding an elaborate painting, "Resources of Wisconsin" by Edwin Blashfield. To obtain the proper perspective, each figure is about thirteen feet high. The

Roman Renaissance motif is carried on throughout the Capitol with elaborate ornamentation and gold-leafed Corinthian pilasters in the Senate and Supreme Court rooms.

State History

Jean Nicolet landed near Green Bay in 1634, the first European to visit the Wisconsin area. He was sent by Samuel de Champlain to make a treaty to trade furs with the Indians. Between 1661, when the Jesuit missionary, Rene Menard came, and 1669, when Father Marquette arrived, Wisconsin was a prime area for Indian missionaries. The first permanent settlers arrived at Green Bay in 1745.

In 1763, the Treaty of Paris ended the French and Indian War, making Wisconsin a British territory. In 1787, it became part of the Northwest Territory; later a part of the Indiana (1800), Illinois (1809), and Michigan (1818) Territories. By 1822, lead mining in southwest Wisconsin brought settlers and miners. The miners were called "badgers" because of their burrowing for lead, and the state became the "Badger State." Agitation with the Indians culminated in the Black Hawk War in 1832. In 1836, Wisconsin became a separate territory.

By 1848, the area's population had grown and all Indian territorial claims were relinquished. On May 29, 1848, Wisconsin joined the Union as the 30th. state. During the Civil War, Wisconsin supported the Union cause with over 90,000 men and over 12,200 casualties. An eagle "Old Abe" was carried into battle as a symbol of the Wisconsin resolve.

State Symbols

Wisconsin's state flower is the wood violet; the state tree, the sugar maple. The state bird is the robin; the state animal, the badger. The state's wild animal is the white-tailed deer; the domestic animal is the dairy cow. Wisconsin's insect is the honey bee; the fish, the muskellunge. The official rock is red granite; the mineral, galena. The official soil is Antigo silt loam; the peace symbol, the mourning dove. "Forward" is the single word motto. The state song is "On Wisconsin." Origins of the word Wisconsin came from: Ouiskousing (Many Waters); Ouiskonsing (Gathering of the Waters; Miskousing or Wis-kansin (Meeting of the Waters).

Wisconsin's State animal, the Badger, is sculptured on a classic pediment over an entryway in the Capitol.

Wyoming

The Equality State; The Sagebrush State

The construction of the Neoclassical Corinthian styled Wyoming State Capitol in Cheyenne was begun in 1886 and completed in 1888. The building is constructed of sandstone from the quarries at Rawlins, Wyoming. The gold-leafed, covered, copper dome of the Capitol rises to 146 feet. It crowns a classical structure that features Corinthian columns and a Roman double portico over the front entrance. The upper porticoes are duplicated on the front of the two wings that were added in 1916.

The interior rotunda is fifty-four feet high to the cathedral glass interior dome. Corinthian columns support each floor of the central interior hall. Most of the woodwork is cherry imported from Sandusky, Ohio. The House and Senate chamber ceilings are of stained glass with the seal of the state of Wyoming in the center. In front of the Capitol is a statue to Esther Hobart Morris who was instrumental in establishing Wyoming as the "Equality State."

State History

The Wyoming area at one time was the possession of France (Louisiana Purchase); Texas (Texas Annexation); British (Oregon Boundary Treaty); Mexico (Mexican Cession); and earlier, Spain. Prior to the 19th. century , few white men had entered the area. Pierre de la Verendrye reached the area in 1743, and some fur traders came into the area earlier. The first organized group to explore Wyoming was led by Wilson Hunt in 1811. Earlier Lewis and Clark neared the area, but did not explore. John Colter with Lewis and Clark explored the Yellowstone Park area about 1807.

By 1835, John Jacob Astor's American Fur Company became the dominant influence in the area. Laramie was the first permanent settlement and a stop on the Oregon Trail. It was John C. Fremont who led a government expedition in 1842-43 that brought the area to the attention of settlers who wished to move westward. The completion of the Union Pacific Railroad in 1867-9 through southern Wyoming brought the pioneers, some of whom settled in the state under the Homestead Act of 1862; others going on to the West coast. The Sioux Indians made peace in 1868, and in 1869, Wyoming became a territory. Cattlemen, sheepherders, and homesteaders fought one another, but eventually settled their differences. Coal, oil, and other resources became important.

On December 10, 1869, Wyoming was the first government in the world to grant women the vote. The National Park system had its beginning in Wyoming with the establishment of Yellowstone Park in 1872. Wyoming became the 44th. state on July 10, 1890.

State Symbols

Wyoming's state flower is the Indian paintbrush; the state bird, the meadowlark. The Plains cottonwood is the Wyoming state tree; the state gem, jade. The state animal is the American bison. The state's motto is "Equal Rights." Wyoming's name comes from the two Delaware Indian words meaning "large plains."

Appendex

Architectural Terms

Architrave The lower most part of an entablature, resting directly on top of a column.

Baluster A short column or post with a base, shaft, and capital usually supporting a top rail.

Balustrade A series or row of balusters with supported railing.

Capital Top portion of a column. The Classic orders are Doric, Ionic, Corinthian, Tuscan, and Composite.

Colonnade A series of columns set at equal intervals.

Colonette A small, decorative column

Cornice A horizontal molding on a wall or the uppermost part of the entablature.

Drum A circular or polygonal wall or other structure supporting the dome. It may have windows. Also one of the cylinders of stone which form a column.

Dentil One of a series of small rectangular blocks forming a molding beneath a cornice.

Entablature A horizontal superstructure resting on the column capitals and made up of an architrave, a frieze (plain or decorated), and a cornice.

Frieze A horizontal band that has decoration. It can be painted around a room or can be sculptured between the architrave and cornice of an entablature.

Pediment In Classical architecture, a wide, low pitched gable end of a building or similar shape over a window or door.

Pilaster A rectangular column with a capital and a base, set into a wall as a decoration.

Portico A porch or covered walk made up of a roof supported by columns.

Tympanum A recessed, ornamental space or panel enclosed by the sloping cornices of a triangular pediment. It may also be undecorated.

Vault An arched structure forming a ceiling or roof.

Above and below are illustrations of architectural terms using examples from the Wisconsin State Capitol in Madison. The inset is the Old Capitol of Iowa on the University of Iowa campus.

1 Pediment 2 Entablature 3 Cornice 4 Frieze 5 Architrave 6 Tympanum
7 Portico 8 Corinthian Capital 9 Doric Capital 10 Ionic Capital 11 Dentil
12 Balustrade.

Alphabetical List and Information on State Capitols

State	City	Completed	Architect(s)	Type
Alabama	Montgomery	1851	Barachias Holt	Greek Revival*
Alaska	Juneau	1931	James A. Wetmore	Office Building
Arizona	Phoenix	1899	James Reily Gordon	Italian Villa Style
Arkansas	Little Rock	1915	George Mann	Classical Revival*
			Cass Gilbert	
California	Sacramento	1878	Reuben Clark	Roman Corinthian*
			Gordon Cummings	
Colorado	Denver	1908	Elijah E. Meyers	Classical Revival*
Connecticut	Hartford	1878	Richard M. Upjohn	Neo-Gothic
Delaware	Dover	1791	Alexander Givan	Colonial
Florida	Tallahassee	1845	Cary Butts	Carpenter built
		1978	Edward D. Stone	Modern Skyscaper
Georgia	Atlanta	1889	Frank Burnham	Roman Renaissance*
			W. J. Edbrooke	
Hawaii	Honolulu	1969	Robert M. Bell	Modern; Stylistic
			Cyril W. Lemmon	
			David Lo	
Idaho	Boise	1919	John E. Tourtellotte	Classical Revival*
Illinois	Springfield	1888	John C. Cochrane	Classical Revival*
			Alfred H. Piquendar	
Indiana	Indianapolis	1878	Edwin May	Roman Renaissance*
			Adolf Scherrer	
Iowa	Des Moines	1886	John C. Cochrane	Neo-Romanesque *
			Alfred H. Piquenard	
Kansas	Topeka	1903	J. C. Haskell	French Renaissance*
Kentucky	Frankfort	1910	Frank M. Andrews	Ionic Revival*
Louisiana	Baton Rouge	1932	Leon Weiss	Modern Skyscraper
			F. Julius Dreyfous	Stylized
			Solis Seiferth	
Maine	Augusta	1832	Charles Bulfinch	Classical Greek*
			Rem: Henri Desmond	
Maryland	Annapolis	1779	Joseph H. Anderson	Colonial
Massachusetts	Boston	1798	Charles Bulfinch	Classical Revival*
Michigan	Lansing	1878	Elijah E. Myers	Classical Revival*
Minnesota	St. Paul	1905	Cass Gilbert	Roman Renaissance*
Mississippi	Jackson	1903	Theodore C. Link	Greek Revival*
Missouri	Jefferson City	1917	Egerton Swartwout	Roman Renaissance*
			Evars Tracy	
Montana	Helena	1902	Charles Emlen Bell	Neoclassical Ionic*
			H. J. Kent	
Nebraska	Lincoln	1930	Bertram G. Goodhue	Modern Skyscraper
Nevada	Carson City	1871	Joseph Gosling	Modern Classical*

State	City	Year	Architect	Style
New Hampshire	Concord	1819	Stewart Park	Roman Renaissance*
New Jersey	Trenton	1889	Jonathan Doan	French Academic*
New Mexico	Santa Fe	1967	W. C. Kruger	Modern Stylistic
New York	Albany	1898	Thomas W. Fuller	Romanesque French
			Arthur Gilman	Gothic
			H. H. Richardson	Modified original
			Leopold Eidlitz	
North Carolina	Raleigh	1840	Ithiel Town	Greek Revival
			Alexander J. Davis	
North Dakota	Bismarck	1934	John Holabird	Modern Office
			John W. Root	
Ohio	Columbus	1861	Alexander J. Davis	Greek Doric Revival
			Isaiah Roberts	
			Ithiel Town	
Oklahoma	Oklahoma City	1917	Wemyss Smith	Greco Roman Revival
			Solomon A. Layton	
Oregon	Salem	1938	Francis Keally	Modern Greek
Pennsylvania	Harrisburg	1906	Joseph Huston	Italian Renaissance*
Rhode Island	Providence	1904	Charles McKim	Classical Revival*
			William Meade	
			Stanford White	
South Carolina	Columbia	1900	John R. Niernsee	Italian Renaissance*
			Frank P. Milburn	Completed Capitol
South Dakota	Pierre	1910	C. E. Bell	Classical Revival*
			M. S. Detwiler	
Tennessee	Nashville	1859	William Strickland	Ionic Greek Revival
Texas	Austin	1888	Elijah E. Myers	Classical Revival*
Utah	Salt Lake City	1915	Richard Kletting	Classical Revival*
Vermont	Montpelier	1859	Thomas W. Silloway	Classical Greek* Revival
Virginia	Richmond	1800	Thomas Jefferson	Doric Greek Revival
Washington	Olympia	1928	Ernest Flagg	Classical Revival*
West Virginia	Charleston	1932	Cass Gilbert	Classical Revival*
Wisconsin	Madison	1909	George B. Post & Son	Greco-Roman Revival*
Wyoming	Cheyenne	1888	David W. Gibbs	Classical Revival*

* Indicates a Domed Capitol

States by Dates of Admission

Original Thirteen Colonies

Delaware	December 7, 1787
Pennsylvania	December 12, 1787
New Jersey	December 18, 1787
Georgia	January 2, 1788
Connecticut	January 9, 1788
Massachusetts	February 6, 1788
Maryland	April 28, 1788
South Carolina	May 23, 1788
New Hampshire	June 21, 1788
Virginia	June 25, 1788
New York	July 26, 1788
North Carolina	November 21, 1789
Rhode Island	May 19, 1790

Establishing a New Nation

Vermont	March 4, 1791
Kentucky	June 1, 1792
Tennessee	June 1, 1796
Ohio	March 1, 1803
Louisiana	April 30, 1812
Indiana	December 11, 1816
Mississippi	December 10, 1817
Illinois	December 3, 1818
Alabama	December 14, 1819
Maine`	March 15, 1820
Missouri	August 10, 1821

Pre-Civil War

Arkansas	June 15, 1836
Michigan	January 26, 1837
Florida	March 3, 1845
Texas	December 29, 1845
Iowa	December 28, 1846
Wisconsin	May 29, 1848
California	September 9, 1850
Minnesota	May 11, 1858
Oregon	February 14, 1859

Civil War Period

Kansas	January 29, 1861
West Virginia	June 20, 1863
Nevada	October 31, 1864
Nebraska	March 1, 1867

Westward Expansion

Colorado	August 1, 1876
North Dakota	November 2, 1889
South Dakota	November 2, 1889
Montana	November 8, 1889
Washington	November 11, 1889
Idaho	July 3, 1890
Wyoming	July 10, 1890
Utah	January 4, 1896
Oklahoma	November 16, 1907
New Mexico	January 6, 1912
Arizona	February 14, 1912

Expansion

Alaska	January 3, 1959
Hawaii	August 21, 1959

The Origins of the States

Alaska

Purchased from Russia in 1867 for $7,200,000. In 1912, Congress established a state government and a representative in Congress.

Arizona

Created from the Gadsden Purchase of land from Mexico. It ratified a state constitution in 1911.

Arkansas

Created from the Louisiana Purchase of 1803, it established a constitution in 1836.

California

Created from land received from Mexico in the Treaty of Guadalope-Hidalgo, California ratified a state constitution on November 13, 1849.

Colorado

The state was created from the Louisiana Purchase and from land received in the Treaty of Guadalope-Hidalgo in 1848 at the end of the Mexican War. A state constitution was ratified in 1876.

Connecticut

It was the fifth state of the original thirteen colonies. A democratic charter called the Fundamental Orders of Connecticut was adopted in 1639. It proclaimed the independence of the colony from England. In 1665, the Connecticut colony was joined by the New Haven colony to form the single colony of Connecticut under a charter from Charles II.

Delaware

It was the first state of the original thirteen colonies. It was settled first by the Dutch based upon Henry Hudson's discovery of Delaware Bay in 1609. Later Swedish settlers occupied the area. It was primarily under the jurisdiction of Pennsylvania until 1776 when a state constitution was enacted.

Florida

Spain ceded the territory of East Florida to U. S. in 1819. Its constitution was set in 1845.

Georgia

It was the fourth colony to ratify the Constitution. In 1732, a charter was granted to James E. Oglethorpe to establish the last of the thirteen colonies on the North American continent. A state constitution was adopted in 1777.

Hawaii

Annexed by the U. S. in 1898, and granted statehood in 1959.

Idaho

Created from the Louisiana Purchase of 1803. A constitution was adopted on November 5, 1889.

Illinois

Created from the Northwest Territory. Adopted a constitution in 1818.

Indiana

Created from the Northwest Territory. Adopted a constitution in 1816.

Iowa

Created from the Louisiana Purchase. Adopted a constitution in 1846

Kansas

Created from the Louisiana Purchase. Adopted a constitution in 1859

Kentucky

Separated from Virginia in 1792. Adopted a constitution in 1891.

Louisiana

Created from the Louisiana Purchase of 1803. Adopted a constitution in 1921 to replace the Civil Code (1808) based upon French and Spanish codes.

Maine

Area from England after the Revolution and a territory established after the War of 1812 in the Treaty of 1814. In 1819, a constitution was drawn up.

Maryland

It was the seventh of the original colonies to ratify the Constitution. In 1632, Charles I of England granted to the Catholic 1st. Lord Baltimore, a charter for land north of the Potomac River. After his death the charter reverted to his son, the 2nd. Lord Baltimore who became the first proprietor. A state constitution was adopted in 1776.

Massachusetts

Massachusetts was the sixth of the original colonies to ratify the Constitution. It was established by the Pilgrims, a group of thirty-five members of the English Leyden group and sixty-six other adventurers from England who landed at Plymouth on December 25, 1620, under the patent of the Virginia Company. A state constitution was ratified by the people in 1790.

Michigan

The Treaty of Paris of 1783 following the Revolution made it part of the U. S. Its first constitution was established in 1835.

Minnesota

Created from land obtained from the Treaty of Paris of 1783 and land from the Louisiana Purchase. A state constitution was adopted in 1857.

Mississippi

Ceded to the U. S. by Spain in 1795. A constitution was adopted in 1817.

Missouri

Created from the Louisiana Purchase of 1803. Organized under the constitution of 1820.

Montana

Created from the Louisiana Purchase of 1803 and the explorations of Lewis and Clark. A state constitution was ratified in 1889.

Nebraska

Created from the Louisiana Purchase of 1803, a constitution was adopted in 1875.

Nevada

Created from land received from Mexico in the Treaty of Guadalupe Hidalgo. A state constitution was ratified in 1864.

New Hampshire

New Hampshire was the ninth colony to ratify the Constitution. In 1622, Captain John Mason received a land grant from the Council for New England for the area that became New Hampshire. It had a permanent provincial government from 1692 until 1776, when a state constitution was adopted.

New Jersey

New Jersey was the third colony to ratify the Constitution. The colony was based upon a 1665 Proprietary Grant to John Lord Berkeley and Sir George Carteret. It was a Royal province from 1701-1738 and under the jurisdiction of the governor of New York. A state constitution was adopted in 1776.

New Mexico

Mexico ceded the area to the U. S. in 1848, and a constitution was adopted in 1911 prior to its admission as a state in 1912.

New York

New York was the eleventh colony to ratify the Constitution on July 25, 1788. The New York area was originally settled by the Dutch following Henry Hudson's voyage up the Hudson River. The Dutch East India Company sent settlers named Walloons in 1621. A state constitution was adopted in 1777.

North Carolina

North Carolina was the twelfth colony to ratify the Constitution on November 21, 1789 The Carolina area below Virginia was granted by Charles I to Sir Robert Heath in 1629. It reverted to the Crown and in 1660, Charles II granted the land to eight Lord Proprietors. A state constitution was adopted in 1776.

North Dakota

Half of the state came from the Louisiana Purchase of 1803 and the rest was ceded to the U. S. by England in the Convention of 1818, that set the U. S. Canadian boundary. A constitution was adopted in 1889.

Ohio

Created a U. S. territory after the Revolution and was part of the Northwest Territory. Congress approved a constitution in 1802.

Oklahoma

Created from the Louisiana Purchase of 1803. The states's constitution was approved in 1907.

Oregon

Occupied by England and U. S. Created from the Oregon Territory in an agreement with England in 1819. Adopted state constitution in 1857.

Pennsylvania

Pennsylvania was the second of the colonies to ratify the Constitution. In 1681, William Penn received a charter from Charles II, naming him as proprietor for the area that included Pennsylvania. In 1776, a state constitution was adopted.

Rhode Island

Rhode Island was the thirteenth state to ratify the Constitution. It was founded by Roger Williams who was driven out of the Massachusetts Bay Colony in 1636. Other dissidents settled in other areas in Rhode Island as well. Rhode Island continued to use the colonial charter of 1662 but deleted all reference to the British crown. The state's constitution was approved in 1842.

South Carolina

South Carolina was the eighth colony to ratify the Constitution. In 1660, Charles II issued charters to eight English noblemen who formed the Carolina colonies. North and South Carolina were separated in 1712. A state constitution was adopted in 1776.

South Dakota

Created from the Louisiana Purchase of 1803. Its constitution was adopted in 1889.

Tennessee

Formed by Congress from land ceded to the U. S. from North Carolina. Its original state constitution was adopted in 1796.

Texas

After Stephen Austin defeat by Mexico at the Alamo, the Republic of Texas under Sam Houston gained statehood. The result was the Mexican War. The state constitution was adopted in 1876.

Utah

Created from land U. S. received in the Treaty of Guadalupe Hidalgo which ended the Mexican War. Its constitution was ratified in 1895.

Vermont

Created from land in dispute by several states following the French and Indian War. New York withdrew its claim to the land in 1789. The state's constitution was adopted in 1777.

Virginia

Virginia became the tenth colony to ratify the Constitution. It was initially founded and named by Sir Walter Raleigh when an expedition sent by him and led by Sir Richard Grenville and Ralph Lane landed on Roanoke Island in July, 1584. The colony eventually failed. In May, 1607, a more permanent settlement was established at Jamestown by the London Company. A state constitution was adopted in 1776.

Washington

The dispute over the area between the English and the U. S. continued after the Louisiana Purchase. The dispute came to an end with the Treaty of 1846 that set the 49th. parallel as the line between Canada and the U. S. Washington's state constitution was adopted in 1889.

West Virginia

During the Civil War, the western settlers of Virginia separated to form a new state that supported the Union. Its constitution is dated 1872.

Wisconsin

Created out of the Northwest Territory. Its constitution was adopted in 1848.

Wyoming

Although many nations had a claim to the area, it was not explored until John Colter, a member of Lewis and Clark Expedition, discovered Yellowstone. It was created from a territory that was established by the migration west of settlers. Its state constitution was ratified in 1889.

Bibliography

Allen, Wm. C. *The Dome of the United States Capitol: An Architectural History* U.S. Government Printing Office, 1992

Bachelis, Faren Maree *The Pelican Guide to Sacramento and the Gold Country* Pelican Publishing Co., Gretna, CA, 1987

Collier's Encyclopedia Crowell-Collier Publishing Co. New York 1956

Daniel, Jean Houston and Price Daniel *Executive Mansions and Capitols of America,* Country Beautiful Foundation, Inc., Waukesha, WI, 1969

Franzen, Marilyn *Capitol Capsules* Bananza Books, 1954

Great Historic Places American Heritage Guide Beverly Da Costa, Ed. American Heritage Publishing Co., New York, 1973

Florida Federal Writers Project, Oxford Press, 1949

Hitchcock, Henry-Russell and William Seale *Temples of Democracy, The State Capitols of the USA* Harcourt Brace Jovanovich, New York and London, 1976

Macmillan Encyclopedia of Architects The Free Press, New York, 1982

Landmarks of the U.S. A.,Our 51 Capitols Home Library Pub. Co., Fort Atkinson, WI, 1976

Paine, Roberta M. *Looking at Architecture* Lothrop, Lee, & Shepard Co., New York, 1974

Roth, Leland R. *A Concise History of American Architecture* Harper and Row, New York, 1979

Shearer, Benjamin F. and Barbara S. Shearer *State Names, Seals, Flags, and Symbols* Greenwood Press, New York, 1987

Sturgis, Russell *A Dictionary of Architecture and Building* Macmillan, London, 1901

White, Norval *The Architecture Book* Alfred A. Knopf, New York, 1976

State Guide Books and Brochures

American Automobile Association State Tour Books

Alaska, the Great Land Office of the Governor, Juneau, Alaska 99811

Arizona State Capitol Museum Arizona Department of Library, Archives and Public Records 1700 W. Washington, Phoenix, Arizona 85007

Colorado State Capitol Colorado Department of Education

Connecticut State Capitol, The Department of Economic Development, 210 Washington Street, Hartford, CT 06106

Connecticut, the Constitution State Department of Economic Development, 210 Washington Street, Hartford, CT 06106

Delaware: *State House: A Preservation Report, The* Delaware Division of Historical and Cultural Affairs, Hall of Records, Dover, DL 19901 1976

Florida's Capitol Center Florida Department of State

Florida: *Short History of Florida, A* Florida Department of State

Florida: *Old Capitol, The* Division of Archives, History, and Records, Florida Department of State

Georgia's Capitol Max Cleland, Secretary of State, 214 State Capitol, Atlanta, GA 30334

Georgia's Official State Symbols Max Cleland, Secretary of State, 214 State Capitol, Atlanta, GA 30334

Hawaii's State Capitol and Government Office of the Governor & Legislature

Hawaii, The Aloha State State of Hawaii and Visitors Bureau

Idaho, The 43rd. State Idaho Travel Council

Idaho State Capitol, Your Visit to the Idaho State Historical Society

Illinois State Capitol Jim Edgar, Secretary of State

Indiana: *The State House, 1888 to Present* Indiana Department of Commerce

Iowa Capitol Guide Public Information Office, Des Moines, Iowa 50319

Kansas Capitol Square Bill Graves, Secretary of State

Kansas Facts Office of Secretary of State Jack Brier
Kentucky's Historic Capitols Kentucky Historical Society, Box H, Frankfort, Ky 40602
Kentucky, the Bluegrass State Kentucky Dept. of Travel Development, Capital Plaza
    Tower, Frankfort, KY 40601
Kentucky, The Traveller's Guide to Kentucky Dept. of Travel Development, Capital Plaza
    Tower, Frankfort, KY 40601
Louisiana, A Dream State Louisiana Office of Tourism, Box 94291, Baton Rouge, La 70804-
    9291
Maine: Earle G. Shettleworth, Jr., and Frank A. Beard *The Maine State House, A Brief
History and Guide* Maine Historic Preservation Commission, Dept. of Economic and
Community Development, Station 59, Augusta, ME 04333
Maryland: *Visit Annapolis and Anne Arundel County*   Tourism Council of Annapolis and
    Anne Arundel County, Inc., 152 Main Street, Annapolis, MD 21401
Maryland State House,The Maine Department of Economic and Community Development,
    Office of Tourism, 1748 Forest Drive, Annapolis,MD 21401
Massachusetts State House,The Office of Secretary of State Michael J. Connolly
Michigan's State Capitol, History, Art, & Architecture Virginia B. Hutcheson, Editor,
Michigan Department of Management and Budget, Capitol Tour Guide and Information
    Service
Michigan Capitol Senator William A. Sederburg
Minnesota State Capitol Minnesota Historical Society, 690 Cedar Street, St. Paul, MN
    55101
Missouri, Facts & Figures Missouri Division of Tourism, Box 1055, Jefferson City, MO 65102
Mississippi, New Capitol State Capitol Commission
Montana Capitol, The Montana Historical Society, Travel Montana, Helena, MT 59620
Nebraska State Capitol Building State Building Div., Lincoln, NE 68509
Nebraska State Capitol, Tower on the Plains NEBRASKAland Magazine, Nebraska Game
    and Parks Commission, & Department of Administrative Services,
    State Building Division, Lincoln, NE 68509
Nevada: *History of Nevada State Capitol and Governor's Mansion* Department of General
    Services, Capitol Complex, Carson City, NV 89710
New Hampshire, The State House-Concord Department of Resources & Economic
    Development, Box 856, Concord, NH 03301
North Carolina State Capitol Travel and Tourism Division, Department of Commerce,
    430 North Salisbury Street, Raleigh, NC 27611
North Dakota State Capitol and Grounds North Dakota Tourism Promotion, 600 E.
    Boulavard, Bismarck, ND 58505
Oklahoma Capitol Complex Oklahoma Tourism and Recreation Department, 500 Will
    Rogers Building, Oklahoma City, OK 73105
Oklahoma: *Discover Oklahoma* Oklahoma Tourism and Recreation Department
    Literature Distribution Ctr., Box 60000, Oklahoma City, OK 73146
Oregon's Capitol Legislative Administration Committee
Pennsylvania State Capitol, The Pennsylvania Dept. of General Services, Harrisburg, PA
Rhode Island State House, The   Office of Public Information, Providence, RI 02903
South Carolina: *The State House* South Carolina Department of Parks, Recreation &
    Tourism, 1205 Pendleton Street, Columbia, SC 29201-3731
South Carolina, Its People and Its History South Carolina Department of Parks,
    Recreation & Tourism, Box 71, Columbia, SC 29202
Tennessee State Capitol   Tennessee Department of Tourist Development, Box 23170,
    Nashville, TN 37202
Texas Capitol Guide State Dept. of Highways and Public Transportation, Austin, TX
Utah, A Guide to Capitol Hill
Vermont: Mary Van Orden *The Vermont State House* Secretary of State Office, Montpelier,
    VT 05602

Virginia State Capitol, The Virginia Division of Tourism, Suite 500, 202 N.Ninth Street, Richmond, VA 23219

Washington State Capitol Offices of the Governor, Secretary of State Legislature, General Administration, Olympia, WA

Washington State Capitol Campus, The Senate and House, State of Washington, Olympia, WA

West Virginia: Ken Hechler *West Virginia State Capitol* Department of Commerce, Capitol Building, Charleston, WV 25305

Wisconsin: Stanley Cravens, (Editor) *Wisconsin State Capitol*

Department of Administration, Division of Buildings and Grounds, Madison, WI 53703

Wisconsin State Capitol Madison, WI 53703

Wyoming: Rick Ewig, Linda G. Rollins & Betty Junge *Wyoming's Capitol*
Archive, Museums, & Historical Depart., Barrett Building, Cheyenne, WY 82002

Index

Order   Form

America's Heritage: Capitols of the United States $9.95 plus $1.75 postage and handling per book.

Please send _____ copies of **America's Heritage: Capitols of the United States.**

Enclosed is a _____check or _____money order.

_____   @ $9.95 = _____

Postage and Handling   1.75

Wis. Residents add 5% Sales Tax   _____

Total   enclosed_____

Send order to :   **State House Publishing**

~~P. O. Box 5636~~   4022 Paunack Ave.
Madison, WI 53711

~~Madison, WI 53705-0636~~

Please complete mailing label. Print or type clearly.

Shipping Label

Name _____

Address _____

City _____ State_____Zip_____

Printed Matter--Books Special Fourth Class
Book Rate or Library Rate
Forwarding & Return Postage Guaranteed
